THE LAST MARTINI

A Hangover Bedside Companion

Such pleasures quickly pass away.

THE EVENING RED.   THE MORNING GRAY.

THE LAST MARTINI

A Hangover Bedside Companion

Compiled by Peter Sellers
with Rob Milling

Library and Archives Canada Cataloguing in Publication

Title: The last martini / compiled by Peter Sellers and Rob Milling.

Names: Sellers, Peter, 1956- compiler. | Milling, Rob, compiler.

Identifiers: Canadiana (print) 20240315367 |
Canadiana (ebook) 20240315421

ISBN 9781771616768 (softcover) ISBN 9781771616775 (PDF)
ISBN 9781771616782 (EPUB) ISBN 9781771616799 (Kindle)

Subjects: LCSH: Hangover—Quotations, maxims, etc. |
LCSH: Alcoholic beverages in literature.

Classification: LCC PN6081 .S45 2024
DDC 808.88/2—dc23

Published by Mosaic Press, Oakville, Ontario, Canada, 2024.
MOSAIC PRESS, Publishers
www.Mosaic-Press.com
Copyright © Peter Sellers 2024
Cover Design: Amy Land

Printed and bound in Canada.

MOSAIC PRESS
1252 Speers Road, Units 1 & 2, Oakville, Ontario, L6L 2X4 (905) 825-2130
info@mosaic-press.com • www.mosaic-press.com

For Jaxon
Read, learn, and beware

CHARACTER

WHERE THERE'S DRINK

THERE'S ALWAYS DANGER

PREVENTION IS BETTER THAN CURE

**It is more glorious to build a Lighthouse
than man a Life-Boat**

Published by The Dominion Scientific Temperance Committee

Temperance Lesson No. 12

In W. S. Van Dyke's 1934 film version of Dashiell Hammett'snovel *The Thin Man*, starring William Powell and Myrna Loy as Nick and Nora Charles, a badly hungover Nora asks her husband, "What hit me?"

Nick replies, "The last martini."

ALCOHOL

A BLESSING

A CURSE

GOOD FOR THE ENGINE, BUT NOT FOR THE
ENGINEER

GOOD FOR COMMERCIAL PURPOSES, BUT NOT AS A BEVERAGE

Published by The Dominion Scientic Temperance Committee.

Contents

The first known written description of a hangover was found in a 3,000-year-old medical textbook *Sushruta-samhita*, written in Sanskrit and published in India. The term used is *paramada*: a post-drinking condition characterized by heaviness, thirst, and pain, with no known cure.

AMOROUS ESCAPADES BACKSTAGE
AND ALONG THE GAY WHITE WAY

(HANGOVER) WILD PARTIES

by MAX LIEF

SPECIALLY REVISED AND EDITED

Introduction

Many summers ago, my friend Rob Milling and I were alone at his family cottage on Sturgeon Lake. In a quest to expand our scientific knowledge, we took a bottle of Rob's father's Adams Antique rye and a large bottle of Coke to mix it with. We drank it all. That led to my first memorable hangover. It also cured me of ever again drinking rye — and of mixing any whiskey with a soft drink.

That experience, and others that followed, caused me to notice how often works of fiction featured scenes of people grappling with hangovers. Often, these scenes were comical, in some cases even hilarious, because hangovers are always funnier when observed from a distance.

The passages turned up everywhere — in fiction of every genre, from novels and stories by the pulpiest of hacks to works by the most revered literary lions. And mention of physical illness brought on by excess proved timeless as well, with references appearing two millennia ago. In this context, the word "hangover" is a relative baby, dating back only to the early 20ᵗʰ century.

The written descriptions ranged from a single sentence to several pages. Not all of them were amusing. Some, like those found in *Last Exit to Brooklyn* and *The Lost Weekend*, were distinctly grim.

Eventually, I started to collect these hangover scenes. Over time my file grew steadily. It didn't just contain excerpts from novels. There were also songs, poems, complete short stories, and scenes from films. At some point, it occurred to me that they might make an enjoyable book.

Fittingly, Rob provided much valuable help with early, pre-internet research, and slowly we accumulated enough material to make a slim volume that we were sure would be a runaway success. The ideal Christmas gift!

That was in the mid-1980s. The manuscript was prepared and sent out, and we waited by the mailbox for the contract to arrive. What came instead were rejection letters from publishers large and small and far and wide.

The letters gave us various reasons for declining the book. More than one told us how difficult it would be to get permissions for the excerpts. Others told us that they had no idea how to market the book. For crying out loud, I thought, nothing could be simpler. I worked in advertising. I could tell them how to market it. But they never asked.

For a while longer, I continued to add to the manuscript but eventually grew resigned to the fact that no one would ever want to publish it. The book lay fallow for almost two decades. Then, one day, I casually mentioned the idea to Howard Aster. Much to my surprise and delight, he loved the idea. So the project was rekindled and finally, forty years after its inception, it's here.

Thanks to Rob Milling for all his help and friendship over several decades; to everybody with whom I ever shared a hangover; and to all the authors, poets, and songwriters who found inspiration in feeling crapulous.

Special thanks to Howard Aster at Mosaic Press for this and many other books since 1987, and to Jaquelin Hollo who did all of the seriously hard work on this baby.

Here it is. Enjoy in moderation.

— Peter Sellers, Toronto, 2024

duntish
adjective:
Mentally incapacitated by a severe hangover.

— Douglas Adams and John Lloyd,
The Meaning of Liff

Who hath woe? who hath sorrow? who hath contentions? who hath babbling? who hath redness of eyes?

They that tarry long at the wine; they that go to seek mixed wine.

Look not upon the wine when it is red, when it giveth its colour in the cup, *when* it moveth itself aright.

At last it biteth like a serpent, and stingeth like an adder.

Thine eyes shall behold strange women, and thine heart shall utter perverse things.

Yea, thou shalt be as he that lieth down in the midst of the sea, or as he that lieth upon the top of a mast.

They have stricken me, *shalt thou say, and* I was not sick; they have beaten me, *and* I felt it not: when shall I awake? I will seek it yet again.

— Proverbs 23:29-35 (King James Version)

"And they say that we are pigs..."

"Awake crapulous in the morning"

The current common meaning of hangover has been in use for little more than one hundred years. Prior to that, for centuries, the most commonly used term was probably crapulous.

Derived from the Latin *crapulos*, by way of the French *crapuleaux*, crapulous was, and remains, although archaic now, a highly versatile word. It has been used to describe both the state of drunkenness and its aftermath. It also could refer to over-indulgence in eating, though that seems to have been a secondary meaning.

Cicero, Plautus, and Livy, among the greatest of Roman writers, all made reference to the drunken headache and nausea that were part and parcel of feeling crapulous.

Famous Roman statesman, philosopher and writer Marcus Tullius Cicero (106 - 43 BC) used the term in an address to the senate:

> *Constitue hoc, consul, aliquando, Brutorum, C. Cassi, Cn. Domiti, C. Treboni, reliquorum quam velis esse causam; edormi crapulam, inquam, et exhala.*

Arrange matters in this way at last, consul; let the cause of the Bruti, of Caius Cassius, of Cnæus Domitius, of Caius Trebonius and the rest be whatever you please it to be: sleep off your hangover, I say, and breathe out.

In English, the term, as cited in the *Oxford English Dictionary*, dates from the mid-sixteenth century to mean "characterized by gross excess in drinking or eating; intemperate; debauched."

The first recorded use of the term in English was in John Bellenden's translation of Hector (Boethius) Boece's *Historia Gentis Scotorum (History of the Scottish People)* in 1536. Bellenden's translation includes the line

"throw their crapulous and shamfull glutone."

By 1755, the meaning had expanded. Samuel Johnson defined it as "suffering from the effects of intemperance in drinking; resulting from drunkenness."

"[Men who] spend their evenings over wine and awake crapulous in the morning."

> — John Campbell, *The Lives of the Lord Chancellors*, 1845

As late as the mid-1960s, the old term still cropped up occasionally, such as in the work of the great, now sadly neglected British novelist Simon Raven.

"At first Daniel was not at all keen to go. In so far as he could make sense of his situation and the new elements of which Percival and Pappenheim had (truthfully or untruthfully?) apprised him, it now seemed more than ever desirable that he should finish up and get out. There was no time for larking about in Hannover and limping home with a crapula."

— Simon Raven, *The Sabre Squadron*, 1966

An interesting variation on crapulous appears in Charles Cotton's 1689 poem *Night Quatrains*.

The drunkard now supinely snores,
His load of ale sweats through his pores,
Yet when he wakes the swine shall find
A cropala remains behind.

Now changed to a noun, and anticipating Raven's use of the word almost 300 years later, cropala forms a link between crapulous and crop-sick, which was another synonym for hungover, a definition first appearing in Nathan Bailey's *An Universal Etymological English Dictionary*, published in 1721.

A fascinating use of this term appears in "A Letter from Dr William Oliver to the Publisher, giving his Remarks in a Late Journey into Denmark and Holland", which appeared in *Philosophical Transactions, Volume XXIII*, published in 1703, predated its appearance in Bailey's dictionary by almost two decades. This description also features an attempt at a cure that is not recommended.

In the year 1685, I was at Konigsburg in Prussia and I saw the knife which was swallowed by a Prussian boor, who, being crop-sick one morning, thrust the haft of his knife down the throat in order to make himself discharge what offended his stomach: from whence it was

taken out by an incision on the left side, a little
below the short ribs, with that success that he
lived several years after it in very good health.

A further connection between crapulous and crop-
sick is the root "crap" which, in sixteenth-century
England, meant the husk of grain or chaff – the resi-
due left behind – which is certainly what a hangover
is. The connection between crap and crop is strength-
ened by the fact that all intoxicating liquor is made
from one form of crop or another: rye, barley, hops,
potatoes, wheat, grapes, and so forth.

As a side note, crapulous, and its many variants,
is probably the source from which the modern term
crap — as in I feel like crap — actually originates. But
enough of that. Let's move on to the word of the day.

Hangover, with its modern meaning, first turned
up in the language in the early 1900s. Its first dictionary appearance was in 1910. Its first appearance in
print, in a work of fiction, was likely in Will Irwin's
1912 novel *The Red Button*.[*]

Two years later, Pulitzer Prize-winning author
Sinclair Lewis used the term in his novel *Our Mr. Wrenn*
when the narrator informs the reader that "I had a
classy hangover."

What follows is a far from comprehensive look at
some of the places and ways in which the word has
turned up since then.

---

[*] See page 81

"A heare of the dog that bote us last night"

Customarily, this applies to a drink taken as a pick-me-up on the morning after a spree, to a drink taken for relief from an excess of drinks. Heywood, in 1546, thus recorded it in his *Dialogue conteynyng prouerbes and epigrammes*: "I pray thee let me and my felow have A heare of the dog that bote vs last night – And bitten were we both to the braine aright." The curious name for the practice comes from a widely accepted medical doctrine that goes back at least to the sixteenth century and was probably the common folk belief many centuries before that. That is, it was generally and seriously believed that if one were bitten by a dog suffering from rabies (by a "mad dog"), one's chance of recovery was greatly improved if a hair from that dog could be secured and bound upon the wound. It may be pertinent to remark that, though this treatment was still recommended up to the middle of the eighteenth century, its efficacy is now doubted; possibly the same could be said of the morning pick-me-up.

— Charles Earle Funk, *A Hog on Ice & Other Curious Expressions*, 1948

"The hair of the dog that gave the wound is advised as an application to the part injured."

— R. Jones, *Treating Canine Madness*, 1760

"I pray the leat me and my felow have A heare of the dog that bote us last night."

— *The Proverbs of John Heywood*, 1546

"Our Ale-knights often use this phrase, Give us a haire of the dog that last bit us."

— *A Dictionarie of the French and English Tongues*, Randle Cotgrave, 1611

I made my way into the bathroom for the ritual ablutions, then continued into the kitchen, pausing to peer out into the outside world. It was all very depressing, so I treated myself to a morning hair-of-the-hound.

— John Brett, *Who'd Hire Brett?*, 1981

"About that," said Hugh, "you shall hear all particulars from me and the great captain conjointly and both together — for see, he's waking up. Rouse yourself, lion-heart. Ha ha! Put a good face upon it, and drink and drink again. Another hair of the dog that bit you, captain! Call for drink! There's enough of gold and silver cups and candlesticks buried underneath my bed," he added, rolling back the straw and pointing to where the ground was newly turned, "to pay for it, if it was a score of casks full. Drink, captain!"

Mr. Tappertit received these jovial prompting with a very bad grace, being much the worse, both in mind and body, for his two nights of debauch, and but indifferently able to stand upon his legs.

With Hugh's assistance, however, he contrived to stagger to the pump; and having refreshed himself with an abundant draught of cold water, and a copious shower of the same refreshing liquid on his head and face, he ordered some rum and milk to be served; and upon that innocent beverage and some biscuits and cheese made a pretty hearty meal. That done, he disposed himself in an easy attitude on the ground beside his two companions (who were carousing after their own tastes), and proceeded to enlighten Mr. Dennis in reference to tomorrow's project.

— Charles Dickens, *Barnaby Rudge*, 1841

Sometimes after a heavy night he had such a headache that he could not drink his coffee, and gave his lessons with heaviness of spirit. For these occasions he kept a few bottles of beer under the bed, and one of these and a pipe would help him bear the burden of life.

"A hair of the dog that bit him," he would say as he poured out the beer, carefully so that the foam should not make him wait too long to drink.

— W. Somerset Maugham, *Of Human Bondage*, 1915

Holtham, with Tom, his engineering companion and friend, headed straight for the Grand Hotel on the Bund and were 'speedily outside a light repast of oysters and Chablis' followed by a game of billiards and a couple of whiskies, doubtless drunk as the hair of the proverbial dog.

— Pat Barr, *The Deer Cry Pavilion*, 1968

Part I

Hangovers of All Shapes and Sizes

"I feel sorry for people who don't drink.
When they wake up in the morning, that's
as good as they're going to feel all day."

— Frank Sinatra

Dixon was alive again. Consciousness was upon him before he could get out of the way; not for him the slow, gracious wandering from the halls of sleep, but a summary, forcible ejection. He lay sprawled, too wicked to move, spewed up like a broken spider-crab on the tarry shingle of the morning. The light did him harm, but not as much as looking at things did; he resolved, having done it once, never to move his eyeballs again. A dusty thudding in his head made the scene before him beat like a pulse. His mouth had been used as a latrine by some small creature of the night, and then as its mausoleum. During the night, too, he'd somehow been on a cross-country run and then been expertly beaten up by secret police. He felt bad.

He reached out for and put on his glasses. At once he saw that something was wrong with the bedclothes immediately before his face. Endangering his chance of survival, he sat up a little, and what met his bursting eyes roused to a frenzy the timpanist in his head.

— Kingsley Amis, *Lucky Jim*, 1954

Unless there was a blizzard on, each of us had a pony to exercise after lunch. All the hung-over at table wanted to know more about the barometric pressure and the low pressure system that was swirling down from the Pole. They didn't care to take some bouncy pony out on to the ice at the end of a jarring rope.

— Thomas Keneally, *A Victim of the Aurora*, 1977

"I rather think it's the other way around," said Causton gently. "Where you find trouble you find a newsman — the trouble comes first." He changed the subject abruptly. "Speaking of Dawson, I find that he's staying at the Imperiale. When Miss Marlowe and I left this morning he was nursing a hangover and breakfasting lightly off one raw egg and the juice of a whisky bottle."

— Desmond Bagley, *Wyatt's Hurricane*, 1966

"Ringling-ringling!" shouted the bedside telephone. When he fumbled the receiver out of its cradle, a familiar voice at the other end of the line said, "We've got a live one, Inspector. Three seventy-one Pagliacci Terrace, Apartment 2C."

Forcing a grunt as close to "I'm on my way" as he could muster, the man in the bed got his feet on the floor and staggered toward the bathroom, hitting a chair and the door-jamb on the way. Grabbing two tight fistfuls of sink porcelain, he stared down at the drain for a long moment. Then he raised his head and saw himself in the mirror. By Jumbo, he looked as bad as he felt! The dead-white skin, the great bloody slash of smile, the huge round maraschino nose, the perfect black triangles of his eyebrows, the dead-white skullcap with the two side-tufts of bright-orange hair. There he was, Clowntown's finest, Inspector Bozo of the Homicide Squad. Talk about a three-ring hangover! Bozo ran the tips of his trembling fingers across his cheek. A trip to Makeup was long overdue. Well, it would have to wait. When Homicide said they had a live one, they meant a dead one.

— James Powell, *A Dirge for Clowntown*, 1989

There was something strange inside his mouth. Clay could feel it. Something very strange. With a groan, he rolled over onto his back. The bed creaked. Instinctively, his hands went to his swollen belly and pressed down. His stomach was bad. But not as bad as his mouth. There was definitely something very strange lurking inside. Lifting his right hand, he dropped it beside his lips. It crept along his face, waiting a chance. Quickly, it reached inside and pulled.

Clay shouted and let go of his tongue. That was it. Someone had done something strange to his tongue. But what? And how? Maybe someone had stolen it. No. That couldn't be. Hadn't he just pulled it with his own hand? He groaned again. Louder. Now he knew. It wasn't his tongue at all. It was his head. His head was spinning. His head...

He sat up quickly, blinking. The room was leaning at a peculiar angle so he pushed against the wall with one hand until it was level. Then he raised both hands to his head and squeezed it. His stomach hurt. Stumbling to his feet, he managed to reach the wall and lean against it, massaging his stomach gently. Lying down was out. No good. But leaning against the wall wasn't much better. Groping for his toilet-article kit, he grabbed his towel and felt his way toward the door. Kicking it open, he stepped outside.

The barracks was quiet. Except for occasional scattered coughing, there was no sound. Holding tight to the wooden banister, Clay crept down the steps to the latrine. The latrine was divided into thirds — showers, toilets and sinks — and he stood, staring from one to the other, undecided on which to use first. The sinks were nearest, so he turned on the cold water spigot and bent down, his mouth wide open. He took a huge swallow. Good. Another swallow. Better. Closing his eyes, he drank until he could feel his stomach swelling. Then he stood and inspected his face in the mirror. There was no doubt about it. He did not look well.

— William Goldman, *Soldier in the Rain*, 1960

There are three different kinds of hangovers. There are hangovers that are green and wet and slimy, full of questions and trembling and the conviction that one has somehow been disemboweled in one's sleep and a recently dead muskrat has been placed where one's stomach used to be. Then there are hangovers that are gray and stony and cold, in which the granite of one's skull has been cracked like the veil of the temple, and the rock of one's brain has been reduced to rubble within, *painful* rubble. And finally there are hangovers that are red and jagged and jolting, lightning bolts shooting in one ear and out the other, more lightning in the elbows and knees, buzzers and electric chairs and whoopee cushions in the stomach, flash bulbs in the eyes, and battery acid in the mouth. Those are the three kinds of hangovers, and Pedro had all three of them.

When he staggered out of the Inter-Air truck into the semidarkness of Jerry's cul-de-sac, Pedro had no memory of the preceding day and could only assume that he was still in Quetchyl and that the city had for some reason been hydrogen-bombed during the night. Surely he was the only survivor, if he could be called in truth a survivor.

"Hii," Pedro said, staggering this way and that over the neat white lines Jerry had drawn on the concrete. "Hii hii hii."

Gradually his staggering led him away from the truck, away from the darkness, up the curving ramp and around the wooden fences toward light and day and —

— Kennedy Airport.

"Hu!" said Pedro. With both hands pressed to his forehead, partially to keep it from exploding and partially to shield his eyes, Pedro squinted in the sunlight and stared out at John F. Kennedy International Airport, New York, New York. A yellow taxicab went by. A bus went by. Taxi-bus-car-car-car-van-taxi-taxi-bus-car-bus-car-car-taxi-van-bus-taxi-taxi went by. Beyond all this sweeping movement swept a broken expanse of intermixed greenery and roadways, fringed by terminal buildings. Sunshine griddled down, turning Pedro's eyes and brain to goat fat.

And bringing memory. Hijack! New York! Gluppe! *Hiiiii*. Pedro staggered backwards into the wooden fence and slowly slid down it until he was seated on the concrete. He was the one who was supposed to be arrested, and José and Edwardo were supposed to get the money and rescue him. Those job assignments made sense; Pedro would be very good at being arrested, and Jose and Edwardo would be very good as rescuers. The other way around made no sense, it was hopeless.

"Hey, brother. What's the problem?"

Pedro was still too befuddled and miserable even to be surprised at having understood the question, which had been spoken in Spanish. Looking, squinting under his protective awning of hands, he saw a smiling round olive face fronted by a bushy black moustache. The fellow was perhaps thirty, short and slender, in an open necked white shirt and black trousers, and a laminated card pinned to his shirt pocket identified him as an employee of Air Canada. He had been on his way to the employee bus stop when he'd noticed Pedro sitting here, and now he said, "You need help or anything?"

"I drank too much," Pedro told him. His throat hurt when he talked.

His new friend laughed, the way people always do when faced with this particular kind of misery. "Hung over, huh?"

— Donald E. Westlake, *Dancing Aztecs*, 1976

Somebody was shaking him. He opened his eyes, to see a black moustache, large and badly trimmed, and it annoyed him so much that he closed his eyes again. "Now then, sir, now then!" it said.

Inigo did not feel called upon to reply.

"Time you was moving if you want the 6:45," it went on.

This remark was so extraordinary that it opened his eyes again. The waiting-room looked quite different in the morning light. He stared at the porter. "Where's Morton Mitcham?" he asked.

The porter shook his head. "'Tain't on this line. I never 'eard of it."

"It's not a station but a man. He was sitting there last night, talking about banjos in Bangkok and conjuring in Singapore. Unless I dreamt it."

"I shouldn't be surprised. I'm a bit that way myself," said the porter earnestly. "Let me 'ave a few or a bit o' tinned salmon last thing, and I'm off, all night. The stuff I've seen! Banjos and Singapore's nothing to it."

"I don't know that I care for Old Rob Roy," Inigo mused. "He's split my head open and left a sort of dark brown taste in my mouth, as if I'd been chewing some of his Highland peat. But look here, where's what's-his-name - wait a minute - Harry Briggs?"

"Ar, now you're talking! You didn't dream '*im*, I can tell you. Went off duty a bit back, he did. You missed the 1:20, didn't you? Going North, aren't you, sir?"

"Am I?" Inigo thought it over. "I suppose so, but before I go anywhere I want a bath and a shave and some health salts in a tumbler of tepid water and then some tea and toast. And perhaps an egg - you never know - one of those young and tender eggs, the little brown ones. Now," and he produced a shilling, "what do you think about that programme?"

"Thank you, sir. Well, what I think is you'd best get on to Grantham on this next train. Dullingham's no good to you, I give you *my* word. Get anything you like at Grantham, anything you like." And the porter smacked his lips at the thought of this roaring metropolis.

So Inigo went to Grantham. He sneaked through the early morning sunshine to the *Angel and Royal*, where he slipped into a bathroom before most of its guests had looked at their early cups of tea, and had to keep several of them at bay because he stayed so long luxuriating in nakedness and warm water. By the time he was fit to appear at the breakfast table, he was ready for anything it had to offer. After breakfast he smoked his pipe and stared, in a rather dreamy fashion, at several newspapers, and it was half-past ten when he finally took the road.

— J.B. Priestley, *The Good Companions*, 1929

He rose abruptly, went to the bathroom and threw up. He tottered back to the bedroom, sat down on the edge of the bed for a moment, his head in his hands. He looked at the clock. Nine-forty-five. He struggled into his bathrobe, rose gingerly, and made his way to the kitchenette with the aid of several pieces of furniture. By great concentration he managed to measure water and coffee into the percolator and set it on the gas plate. With this hope in view he was able to withdraw a jar of tomato juice from the refrigerator and pour out a glass, which he drank in small sips. The coffee began to bubble into the little glass dome. He waited as long as he could, then poured out a cupful. He staggered into the living-room, slopping the coffee into the saucer. It was a terrible day — the sky was black, the rain pouring. Also, he couldn't see things very well — ah, no wonder, he had forgotten to put on his glasses. He debated the possibility of going into the bedroom to get them, then leaned his head against the back of the chair and closed his eyes. But then the floor began to rock; he was obliged to open them again and drink a large swallow of coffee, which burned his tongue and throat. In response to this attack, his stomach gave a heave, but then subsided. He was able to turn his attention to less tangible effects of debauchery — guilt, shame, and mocking laughter.

He had made a fool of himself, an awful fool. He who hesitates is lost, his mind regurgitated. Faint heart never won fair maiden. Opportunity knocks but once. Fools rush in where angels fear to ... How happy he had been last evening before going out ... how miserably, idiotically happy. It seemed life was conspiring to teach him that happiness for him was only a prelude to ... Pride goeth before a fall. Was it pride? No, it seemed to him he had always been reasonably humble. What he had been proud of were real, tangible accomplishments — a Phi Beta Kappa key, a PhD ... His father had always said his mother spoiled him. Praise to the face sure disgrace. All the adages of his childhood were coming back to him in gusts, like reminders of an undigested meal. He should never have drunk so much — oh, he knew a great deal better than to drink so much, with the kind of stomach *he* had!

— Helen Eustis, *The Horizontal Man*, 1946

The crew came back from Fort Worth hung over and subdued. Jasper Fant's head was splitting to such an extent that he couldn't bear to ride — he got off his horse and walked the last two miles, stopping from time to time to vomit. He tried to get the other boys to wait on him — in his state he could have been easily robbed and beaten, as he pointed out — but his companions were indifferent to his fate. Their own headaches were severe enough.

"You can walk to China for all I care," Needle said, expressing the sentiments of the group. They rode on and left Jasper to creep along as best he could.

Po Campo had anticipated their condition and had a surprise waiting for them — a sugary cobbler made with dewberries he had picked.

"Sugar is the thing for getting over liquor," he said. "Eat a lot and then lie down for a few minutes."

"Did Jasper quit?" Call asked.

"No, he's enjoying the dry heaves somewhere between here and town," Soupy Jones allowed. "Last I heard of him he sounded like he was about to vomit up his socks."

"What's the news of Jake?" Call inquired.

The question produced a remarkable collection of black looks.

"He's a haughty son of a bitch," Bert Borum said. "He acted like he never knowed a one of us."

"He tolt me I smelled like cowshit," Needle said. "He was sitting there gambling and had some whore hanging over him."

"I wouldn't say he misses that one that got took," Soupy said.

Jasper Fant finally straggled in. Everyone was standing around grinning, though he couldn't see why.

"Something must have happened funnier than what I been doing," he said.

"A lot of things are funnier than vomiting," Pea Eye said.

"Jasper missed the cobbler, that's the laugh," Allen O'Brien said, not feeling too frisky himself. "I used to be better at hangovers, back in Ireland. Of course, then I had one every day," he reflected. "I had more practice."

When Jasper realized he had missed a dewberry cobbler, one of his favorite dishes, he threatened to quit the outfit, since they were so ungrateful. But he was too weak to carry out his threat. Po Campo forced him to eat a big spoonful of molasses as a headache cure, while the rest of the crew got their herd on the move.

"I guess the next excitement will be the old Red River," Dish Boggett said, as he took the point.

— Larry McMurtry, *Lonesome Dove*, 1985

Yoshiya woke with the worst possible hangover. He could barely open one eye; the left lid wouldn't budge. His head felt as if it had been stuffed with decaying teeth during the night. A foul sludge was oozing from

THE LAST MARTINI | 13

his rotting gums and eating away at his brain from the inside. If he ignored it, he wouldn't have a brain left. Which would be all right, too. Just a little more sleep: that's all he wanted. But he knew it was out of the question. He felt too awful to sleep.

He looked for the clock by his pillow, but it had vanished. Why wasn't it there? No glasses, either. He must have tossed them somewhere. It had happened before.

Got to get up. He managed to raise the upper half of his body, but this jumbled his mind, and his face plunged back into the pillow. A truck came through the neighbourhood selling clothes-drying poles. They'd take your old ones and exchange them for new ones, the loudspeaker announced, and the price was the same as twenty years ago. The monotonous, stretched-out voice belonged to a middle-aged man. It made him feel queasy, but he couldn't vomit.

The best cure for a bad hangover was to watch a morning talk show, according to one friend. The shrill witch-hunter voices of the showbiz correspondents would bring up every last bit left in your stomach from the night before.

But Yoshiya didn't have the strength to drag himself to the TV. Just breathing was hard enough. Random but persistent streams of clear light and white smoke swirled together inside his eyes, which gave him a strangely flat view of the world. Was this what it felt like to die? OK. But once was enough. Please, God, never do this to me again.

"God" made him think of his mother. He started to call out to her for a glass of water, but realized he was home alone. She and the other believers had left for Kansai three days ago. It takes all kinds to make a world: a volunteer servant of God was the mother of this hangover heavyweight. He couldn't get up. He still couldn't open his left eye. Who the hell could he have been drinking so much with? No way to remember. Just trying turned the core of his brain to stone. Never mind now: he'd think about it later.

— Haruki Murakami, *After the Quake*, 2002

"This morning," she began slowly, "I woke up in that miserable little hotel room with a hangover to end them all. God, I felt rotten! I could remember everything pretty well...you going down to the bus station with me, getting the room and so on, but the rest of the day was nothing. Did you ever get like that?"

My head was vibrating like a struck gong and my stomach was full of fluttering, little winged creatures. Every muscle of my body ached and all I wanted to do was stay in bed and quietly nurse my hangover.

— Charles Willeford, *Pick-Up*, 1955

"As It Used To Be of a Morning"
By Don Marquis

Well, I promised I would tell just what those vanished barrooms was like, and I will tell the truth, so help me.

One thing that I can't get used to going without is that long brass railing where you would rest your feet, and I have got one of them fixed up in my own bedroom now so when I get tired setting down I can go and stand up and rest my feet one at a time.

Well, you would come in in the morning and you would say, Ed, I ain't feeling so good this morning.

I wonder what could the matter be, Ed says, though he has got a pretty good idea of what it could be all the time. But he's too kind hearted to let on.

I don't know, you says to Ed, I guess I am smoking too much lately. When you left here last night, Ed says, you seemed to be feeling all right, maybe what you got is a little touch of this here influenza.

It ain't influenza, Ed, you says to him, it is them heavy cigars we was all smoking in here last night. I swallered too much of that smoke, Ed, and I got a headache this morning and my stomach feels kind o' like it was a democratic stomach all surrounded by

15

republican voters, and a lot of that tobacco must of got into my eyes and I feel so rotten this morning that when my wife said are you going downtown without your breakfast I just said to her Hell and walked out to dodge a row because I could see she was bad tempered this morning.

What would you say to a little absinthe, says Ed, sympathetic and helpful, a cocktail or frappy.

No, says you, if you was to say what I used to say, I leave that there stuff to these here young cigarette-smoking squirts, which it always tasted like paregoric to me.

Yes, sir, Ed says, it is one of them foreign things, and how about a milk punch, it is sometimes soothing when a person has smoked too much.

No, Ed, you says, a milk punch is too much like vittles and I can't stand the idea of vittles.

Yes, sir, Ed used to say, you are right, sir, how about a gin fizz. A gin fizz will bring back your stomach to life right gradual, sir, and not with a shock like being raised from the dead.

Ed, you says to him, or leastways I always used to say, a silver fizz is too gentle, and one of them golden fizzes, with the yellow of an egg in it, has got the same objections as a milk punch, it is too much like vittles.

Yes, sir, Ed says, I think you are right about vittles. I can understand how you feel about not wanting vittles in the early part of the day. And that makes you love Ed, for you meet a lot of people who can't understand that. There ain't no sympathy and understanding left in the world since bartenders was abolished.

How about an old-fashioned whiskey cocktail, says Ed.

You feel his is getting nearer to it, and you tell him so, but it don't seem just like the right thing yet.

And then Ed sees you ain't never going to be satisfied with nothing till after it is into you and he takes the matter into his own hands.

I know what is the matter with you, he says, and what you want, and he mixes you up a whiskey sour and you get a little cross and say it helped some but there was too much sugar in it and not to put so much sugar in the next one.

And by the time you drink the third one, somewhere away down deep inside of you there is a warm spot wakes up and kind of smiles.

And that is your soul has waked up.

And you sort of wish you hadn't been so mean with your wife when you left, and you look around and see a friend and have one with him and your soul says to you away down deep inside of you for all you know about them old Bible stories they may be true after all and maybe there is a God and kind of feel glad there may be one, and if your friend says let's go and have some breakfast you are surprised to find out you could eat as egg if it ain't too soft or ain't too done.

Well, I promised, so help me, I would tell the truth about them barrooms that has perished away, and the truth I will tell, and the truth with me used to be that more than likely it wasn't really cigars that used to get me feeling that way in the morning.

— Don Marquis, *The Old Soak*, 1921

That Would Be Great
If Only It Really Worked

"The only cure for a real hangover is death."

— Robert Benchley

It was nine-fifteen by the time I walked into the Stanford Court, but that didn't matter because Littlejohn was also fifteen minutes late. We ran into each other in the middle of the lobby.

He was a short, round, middle-aged guy who wore flashy clothes made for somebody half his age and a couple of pounds of gold jewelry, most of it around his neck. This morning he had on lemon-yellow trousers, a ruffled pink shirt open at the throat, a paisley neck scarf, and a mod-type, off-white jacket with tight sleeves that ended halfway up his forearms. All of the clothing was wrinkled and baggy, whether on purpose or not I had no idea. His hair was even bushier than I remembered it, and so black he might have died it with shoe polish. At his best he looked like one of the Three Stooges in a Mack Sennett two-reeler. Today he was not at his best. Today his eyes were blood-filled and sunken deep inside puffy hollows, his face had a swollen look, his appendages trembled, and he walked the way a man might if he were barefoot on a bed of hot coals. Hangover with a capital H.

The Stanford Court is a very ritzy, conservative Nob Hill hotel, even more exclusive than the Mark Hopkins and the Fairmont nearby. Well-dressed citizens, most of them past fifty, stared warily at Littlejohn as if they thought he might suddenly become violent. They stared at me, too, when he threw one arm around my shoulders and used his other hand to squeeze mine like a grocery shopper squeezing a peach to see if it was ripe. He also breathed on me, which made it difficult for me not to throw up on him. He had a breath like a goat with pyorrhea.

"Oh, baby," he said in rueful tones, "I got a head big as a watermelon. Goddamn booze. Sometimes I think I should have kept on doing coke, never mind what happened to guys like Belushi. At least you don't wake up with a head like the Goodyear blimp and a taste in your mouth like some dog took a dump on your tongue."

An aristocratic lady in furs heard that, gasped delicately, and then cut him up with a glare like a laser beam. He didn't even know she existed. I tried offering her a small, apologetic smile, but she curled her lip at me. Guilt by association.

"It was worth it, though, kid," Littljohn said. He had hold of my arm now — the way Kerry holds it when we're walking together — and was steering me toward the restaurant. "I got a couple of sugar daddies lined up. *Mucho* bucks. Last night it was fast serves and hot volleys; now the ball's in their court. But the linesman's on our side and we'll get the call, I feel it in my gut. You know what I mean?"

"Sure," I said. I had no idea what the hell he was talking about.

The restaurant wasn't crowded, but it took a few minutes for us to get a table. I think that was because there was a discreet discussion among the staff as to the advisability of seating somebody who looked like one of the Three Stooges with a hangover. Two different employees asked him if he was a guest of the hotel, as if they couldn't believe the management had been so lax. When he finally did get a table, it was at the rear and well removed from any of the other patrons.

A cherubic blond waitress appeared, looking as wary as the people out in the lobby. She couldn't keep her eyes off Littlejohn; she may have thought she was hallucinating. At length she asked him, "Black coffee for you, sir?"

He pulled a face. "Christ, no. Tell you what I want, sweetheart. Three cinnamon buns, the frosted kind. Big ones. Six bananas, cut up in a bowl, no milk or cream. And a couple of bottles of Amstel lager."

She just looked at him. So did I. Pretty soon she said, tentatively, "Are you making some kind of joke?"

"Do I look like I'm joking? I'm in pain, sweetie."

"Three cinnamon buns, six bananas, and...two bottles of beer?"

"Amstel lager. Right."

"All just for you? For *breakfast?*"

"Right, right. Give my man here whatever he wants."

She shifted her gaze to me, not without reluctance. I eased her mind some by ordering coffee, orange juice, and an English muffin. She wrote that down, stared some more at Littlejohn, and went away looking dazed.

Littlejohn leaned toward me, as if he were about to impart a great truth. "Glucose," he said.

"Uh...pardon?"

"Glucose, baby. That's the secret."

"Of what?"

"Life. Yours and mine — everybody's. We're like cars and glucose is our high octane unleaded. Capeesh?"

"Glucose," I said, nodding.

"Too much booze, see, that sends the old corpus into a glucose depression. So the first thing you got to do the morning after, you got to build your glucose level back up. That's what the cinnamon buns are for. Lots of sugar, see?"

"Lots of sugar."

"Right. The bananas, they're for serotonin and norep. Norep, that's short for norepinephrine. The booze knocks down your serotonin and boosts up your norep. Adrenaline is what puts 'em back in balance, so you got to give the old adrenals a kick in the ass to get them producing. Gorilla fruit is the ass-kicker."

"Ass-kicker," I said.

"Right. And the beer, that's how you rebalance your screwed up electrolytes. Beer's loaded with sodium and potassium, right? And what it *also* does, it manufactures urine. *That* washes all the alcohol poisons out of your system." He leaned back and spread his hands. "You see how the whole thing works?"

"Sure," I said. I had no idea what the hell he was talking about.

He nodded vigorously, winced, and nodded again much less vigorously. "Sure. I got the poop from this med student wanted to write screenplays. Lousy screenplays but he sure as hell knows his chemistry. Works like a charm. Eat those buns and bananas, drink the beer, go take a leak, and *voila!* you're a new man."

This was going to be a long breakie, I thought. This was probably going to be the longest breakie of my life.

Littlejohn didn't want to talk business until his serotonin was down and his norep was up and his adrenals had been kicked in the ass; so we sat there and waited for the waitress, and after she came I sat there and watched Littlejohn hunch over his cinnamon buns and bananas and beer like a gaudy vulture over a road kill. The spectacle was such that I had no appetite for my English muffin and managed to get only half the orange juice down. After he was done eating he belched, not too loud, and went off to take the leak that would make him a new man. When he came back the new man looked as hungover as the old one, except that it was grinning. He sat down again, leaned toward me, and imparted his big news in the same great-truth tone he had used to tell me about glucose.

"Eldorp," he said.

At first I thought he'd belched again. I just stared at him.

But it wasn't a belch; it was a name. "Frankie Eldorp," he said.

— Bill Pronzini, *Jackpot*, 1990

"Wake up! Wake up," Anna said, shaking him gently. "Zeiger's here. It's important. Wake up!"

Sidnitz opened his eyes and looked into Anna's face. "Mmm? What time is it?"

"Nine o'clock," she said.

"It's dark," he said.

"Yes. It's Saturday night. Come on, wake up."

He sat up on his elbows. "What's the trouble?"

"Melina Anido has died. Zeiger's here for you. For the *minyon*."

"Oh, God! Can't Benno go?"

"Benno's in Pancheros and, anyway, he won't find ten Jews in El Pueblo."

"Well, then. There's no need to go." He lay down again. She shook him. "You've *got* to go. It's your duty!" she said.

He turned to her. "Leave me alone! Leave me alone!"

"God, you've got a hangover," she muttered. "Here, I've brought some black coffee. I thought you might need it." She poured him some coffee.

"Go away," he said. "I feel ill."

"Don't be a child," she said. "Drink this."

"Look – I don't want to be involved with Anido, with Zeiger, with you, with anybody. I don't want to be involved." He coughed and spluttered violently. "I'm ill. Now go away."

"It's your duty," she said firmly.

"Will you get the hell out of here?"

"He has to get the body to Palemno. It's your duty to be with him. As a Jew!"

There was a knock on the door and Zeiger came in. "Aren't you up yet?"

"Go away."

Anna said to Zeiger: "He's got a bad hangover."

Zeiger burst out laughing and walked into the bathroom. He ran the cold tap and held a towel under it. He came back into the room and looked down at Sidnitz.

"There's one thing I know how to cure," Zeiger said. "A hangover!" He threw the wet towel onto Sidnitz's face and Sidnitz shot up in the bed.

"What the hell do you think you're doing?" he shouted.

"You see?" the doctor said. "Infallible. Now get out of bed. We've got to bury somebody."

— Ronald Harwood, *The Guilt Merchants*, 1963

When Mr. Sermon opened one eye the first thing he saw was a woman's dress. It was empty and suspended on a hanger that was hooked to the picture-rail a yard from the narrow bed in which he lay. He studied it objectively, noting the cellophane sheath in which it reposed and the broad lace collar with exaggerated points that reminded him of the shirt stained with Charles I blood that he had seen in the United Services Museum, in Whitehall.

He studied the dress for more than a minute, deciding that it was too loud and flouncy for his taste but it was not until his single eye roved along the wall towards the window and observed other items of female clothing piled on a chair, that he related the garment to his present whereabouts and wondered what on earth he could be doing in a bed within reach of such things. Then, like a douche of ice-cold water, the two streams of thought mingled and poured over him and he jerked himself upright, gazing round the little room with amazement and alarm.

He did not recognise it or anything in it. It was neatly and simply furnished with a small wardrobe, a bedside table, a small rug laid on patterned linoleum and cretonne curtains that were half-drawn, but apart from the items of clothing there was nothing whatever to give it an identity. Sebastian at last opened the other eye, which seemed to have been gummed up during the night and was reluctant to view the day-light. He then saw his own rucksack, which brought him a little comfort for it was the only familiar object in the room, and then, with both eyes open, he rec-ognised his clothes, neatly folded and placed on a stool near the wardrobe. Like a swimmer far out to sea who has sighted a distant vessel, he projected himself upward and outward from the bed, giving a kind of yelp and springing on to the cold linoleum to dive for his trousers. It was only when he had fished out his wallet and found his money intact that he realised he was wearing nothing but his short cotton underpants and as though escaping from a burning building he plunged into his trousers, fastened them with trem-bling fingers and began a minute inspection of the room, half his attention on what he found and half engaged in a desperate grapple to reconstruct his last conscious period.

He remembered arriving at a pub with a ridicu-lous name, 'The Dove and Donkey' or 'The Dog and Dove' — no, that wasn't is proper name, it was some-thing much more staid, the Something Arms, an old coaching hostelry approached by a narrow arch that led to the cobbled yard. He ran across to the little window and looked out. There was the identical yard and he was now looking down on it from a great height. He then remembered the party and rivers of beer, and himself roaring out choruses at the piano and a game of darts and then...? He darted across and looked at himself in the mirror and saw that he needed a shave but apart from this his face looked familiar, a little drawn and bug-eyed perhaps, but not noticeably different from the narrow, thoughtful face he inspected every morning whilst shaving. It then occurred to him that he should have a hangover, surely a terrible hangover after all that draught beer consumed in that smoke-laden atmosphere, but he had no hangover, not a trace of one and the certainty that he had not helped to restore his confidence so that he said, aloud: "This is a rum do! Where the devil am I? A hotel, certainly, and the hotel Tapper took me to last evening but is whose room? Obviously not my own but somebody else's, a perfect stranger's!"

Then his eyes moved from the suspended pink dress to the pile of clothing on the chair and he reached out and picked up one of the garments, dropping it as though it was a live snake when he realised what it was, a pair of white, silk panties, with blue lover's knots embroidered on the hem. After that he began to panic. His mouth felt dry and his heart pounded so mercilessly that it hurt his ribs and he felt sick with apprehension. He looked carefully at the bed, relieved to discover that it had but one pillow upon which was the imprint of his head and nobody else's. The discovery steadied him somewhat so he was able to cross over to the marble-topped washstand and pour water into the china bowl and slop it round his face and over his neck and ears. Then he found his toilet bag in the rucksack and gave himself a proper wash. He put on his vest and shirt and was in the act of pulling on his socks when he heard the pleasant rattle of china outside the door and then a gentle double-knock that sounded to Mr. Sermon like an impersonal summons to the guillotine.

"Co...come in!" he squeaked, and the door opened to reveal a smiling Bella, with a small tea-tray skillfully balanced in the crook of her elbow.

"Hullo, Professor!" she said cheerily, "I thought you might like some tea. No extra charge. No charge at all in fact. Sleep well?" She indulged herself in a little giggle. "I'll bet you did! You was out cold when I laid you there, never moved a muscle you didn't." She glanced at the bed. "Tidy sleeper, too! There now, shall I pour you a cup?"

"Er...do...please!" stuttered Mr. Sermon, overwhelmed by her breezy warmth, and then, "I say, Bella — it is Bella, isn't it? Exactly where am I? I mean, whose room is this?"

"It's mine," she said, apparently surprised by the question, "whose should it be?"

"*Yours!*" He jumped up, stuffing his shirt into his trousers with frantic haste. "But Good Lord — I mean — how, why?"

She laughed and pushed him down on the bed.

"Here, drink it down. I bet you're parched but I'll also lay odds you haven't got a hangover, have you now?"

"No, I haven't," admitted Mr. Sermon, "but I...I should have, never in my life have I drunk as much as I did last night!"

"Well, you've got me to thank for *that*!" she said triumphantly. "Tapper said don't bother but I came back when he'd gone, lifted you up and made you drink it. You did, too, like a lamb. It's my special, Worcester Sauce base, dash of milk and egg yolk, with two Codeine dissolved separit and added."

"It's very good of you, I'm sure," said Sebastian.

— R.F. Delderfield, *The Spring Madness of Mr. Sermon*, 1963

I shall always remember the morning he came. It so happened that the night before I had been present at a rather cheery little supper, and I was feeling pretty rocky. On top of this I was trying to read a book Florence Craye had given me. She had been one of the house-party at Easeby, and two or three days before I left we had got engaged. I was due back at the end of the week, and I knew she would expect me to have finished the book by then. You see, she was particularly keen on boosting me up a bit nearer her own plane of intellect. She was a girl with a wonderful profile, but steeped to the gills in serious purpose. I can't give you a better idea of the way things stood than by telling you that the book she'd given me to read was called *Types of Ethical Theory*, and that when I opened it at random I struck a page beginning:

> The postulate or common understanding involved in speech is certainly co-extensive, in the obligation it carries, with the social organ-ism of which language is the instrument, and the ends of which it is an effort to subserve.

All perfectly true, no doubt; but not the sort of thing to spring on a lad with a morning head.

I was doing my best to skim through this bright little volume when the bell rang. I crawled off the sofa and opened the door. A kind of darkish sort of respectful Johnnie stood without.

"I was sent by the agency, sir," he said. "I was given to understand that you required a valet."

I'd have preferred an undertaker; but I told him to stagger in, and he floated noiselessly through the doorway like a healing zephyr. That impressed me from the start. Meadowes had had flat feet and used to clump. This fellow didn't seem to have any feet at all. He just streamed in. He had a grave, sympathetic face, as if he, too, knew what it was to sup with the lads.

"Excuse me, sir," he said gently.

Then he seemed to flicker and wasn't there any longer. I heard him moving about in the kitchen, and presently he came back with a glass on a tray.

"If you would drink this, sir," he said, with a kind of bedside manner, rather like the royal doctor shooting the bracer into the sick prince. "It's a little preparation of my own invention. It is the Worcester Sauce that gives it its colour. The raw egg makes it nutritious. The red pepper gives it its bite. Gentlemen have told me they have found it extremely invigorating after a late evening."

I would have clutched at anything that looked like a lifeline that morning. I swallowed the stuff. For a moment I felt as if someone had touched off a bomb inside the old bean and was strolling down my throat with a lighted torch, and then everything seemed suddenly to get all right. The sun shone in through the window; birds twittered in the tree-tops; and, generally speaking, hope dawned once more.

"You're engaged!" I said, as soon as I could say anything.

I perceived clearly that this cove was one of the world's workers, the sort no home should be without.

"Thank you, sir. My name is Jeeves."

— P.G. Wodehouse, *Carry On, Jeeves*, 1925

I pressed the button that read Dr. H. Pine. It seemed to release a battery of chimes that were worthy of Notre Dame. Even *I* winced, but from inside I could hear something that sounded like a cry of pain. There was a moment until the chimes exhausted themselves, then slowly the door opened.

To put it briefly, Dr. Pine looked even worse than I did. His skin was green under his day-old beard. His bathrobe hung like an old sack, his feet were in scuffs. His hair looked like some birds had started to build a nest in it, then changed their minds. He held a dripping ice pack in one hand and an egg in the other.

The two of us stood there for a moment, just looking, appalled at each other's appearance.

"Come in," he said sourly.

Inside, the curtains were drawn to dim the daylight. Pine closed the door and again we just looked at each other. Now that I was here, I couldn't think of a damned thing to say. I finally asked him if he had a hangover.

He looked at me with as much disdain as he could manage. "Calling what I have a hangover is like referring to the Johnstown Flood as a slight drizzle."

"Sorry," I said.

"I'll bet."

"I don't feel too good myself."

He peered at me through bloodshot eyes. "Is that what you came to tell me?"

"No, I - I - I found myself at a bit of a loss. I'm sorry you missed that eight o'clock class."

He put the ice pack gingerly to his head. "I may miss the whole semester."

He followed my gaze down to the egg in his hand.

"Oh," he remembered, "I was making something." He shuffled to the kitchen, losing one of his scuffs en route.

I picked up the scuff and followed him into the kitchen.

It was one of those bachelor kitchens, small but efficient, the coffee pot bubbling merrily on the stove. Pine shushed it pleadingly as he turned off the gas. Then he went over to the counter and resumed mixing some concoction he'd been working on.

I remembered I was holding his scuff. "You lost this," I said and I dropped it near his foot. It struck the floor with a bang. Pine winced, closing his eyes tightly. I made a gesture of apology.

"What're you doing here anyway?" he said irritably.

"Well..." I started uncertainly. The fumes from the coffee pot were tantalizing. "Mind if I have some coffee?"

"If you don't rattle the cups and saucers," he said.

"Thanks."

I proceeded to help myself to some black coffee as Pine worked away on his mixture. Maybe I don't remember it clearly, but I could swear that as I stood there he added some sauerkraut juice, an egg with part of the shell, four anchovies, Tabasco, chili powder, and a few other uncertain ingredients.

"Morning-after specialty?" I asked, sipping my coffee gratefully.

He nodded. "This recipe was given to me by an anthropologist. It's a mixture used by a tribe of cannibals in the Melanesia Islands. They drink this brew whenever they eat a poisoned enemy. Of course, it really should be made with lizard eggs." He shrugged. "But you can't have everything." He looked around for another egg. "Now, what do you want?"

"Well, uh…" I started.

"Please don't shout," he said.

"I wasn't shouting."

"To my ears, at the moment," he said, "you sound like a parade of Banshees."

He dropped another egg in the direction of the mixture, didn't quite make it, the yolk plopping to the floor. He started to bend down, but that was unthinkable, so he shoved the egg under the counter with his foot.

"I still can't understand it," he said, shaking his head and reaching for another egg. "That bartender must have switched to some cheap liquor."

By now I was in the throes of self-analysis. "What *do* I want? What *am* I doing here, now that you mention it?"

Pine was busy with his own dilemma. "My mental control was worked out perfectly," he mused. "Ten years of drinking and it's never failed. There's got to be a logical explanation."

"I must know five thousand people," I went on. "Maybe a thousand by their first names. And you're the only one I can think of to talk to — about something like this."

"What?" he asked, suddenly aware that I was saying something.

"You're an authority on human behaviour," I said. "Maybe you can —"

"Authority!" he snorted. "I thought so until last night."…Pine stopped stirring his concoction, raised it to his lips. But the sight and smell of it were obviously so nauseating that he poured it down the sink instead.

— Fay and Michael Kanin, *Teacher's Pet* (A novelization based on their original screenplay), 1958

Next day I woke up with a headache, vaguely recalling the events of the day before. My reflections were interrupted by Savelyich, who came in to me with a cup of tea.

"It's early you have taken to drinking, Pytor Andreyvish," he said to me, shaking his head, "much too early. And whom do you get it from? Neither your father nor your grandfather were drunkards; and your mother, it goes without saying, never tastes anything stronger than kvass. And who is at the bottom of it all? That damned Frenchman. He kept running to Antipyevna: 'Madame, she voo pree vodka.' Here's a fine 'she voo pree' for you! There is no gainsaying it, he has taught you some good, the cur! And much need there was to hire an infidel for a tutor! As though Master had not enough servants of his own!"

I was ashamed. I turned away and said to him: "Leave me, Savelyich, I don't want any tea." But it was not easy to stop Savelyich once he began sermonizing.

"You see now what it is to take too much, Pytor Andreyvich. Your head is heavy, and you have no appetite. A man who drinks is no good for anything... have some cucumber brine with honey or, better still, half a glass of homemade brandy. Shall I bring you some?"

— Alexander Pushkin, *The Captain's Daughter and Other Stories*, 1936

Hungover Aboard
The African Queen

Hangovers can change from one medium to another. To demonstrate the point, here's the famous hangover scene from C.S. Forester's The African Queen. *First, as Forester originally wrote it and then in an excerpt from James Agee's lyrical screenplay for John Huston's popular 1951 film version starring Katherine Hepburn and Humphrey Bogart.*

Dawn revealed to her Allnutt lying like a corpse on the floorboards. His face, hardly veiled by the sprouting beard, was a dirty grey, and from his open mouth came soft but unpleasing sounds. There was no pleasure in the sight of him. Rose got to her feet and stepped over him; she would have spurned him with her foot save that she did not want to rouse him to violent opposition to what she was going to do. She dragged out the case of gin, took out a bottle and stripped the lead foil from the end. The cork was of the convenient kind which needs no corkscrew. She poured the stuff overside, dropped the bottle in after it, and began on another.

When for the third time the glug-glug-glug of poured liquid reached Allnutt's ears he muttered something, opened his eyes, and tried to sit up.

"Jesus!" he said.

It was not the sight of what Rose was doing which called forth the exclamation, for he still did not know the reason of the noise which had roused him. Allnutt's head was like a lump of red-hot pain. And it felt as if his head, besides, were nailed to the floorboards, so that any attempt at raising it caused him agony. And his eyes could not stand the light; opening them intensified the pain. He shut his eyes and moaned; his mouth was parched and his throat ached, too.

Allnutt was not a natural-born drinker; his wretched frame could not tolerate alcohol. It is possible that his small capacity for liquor played a part in the unknown explanation of his presence in German Central Africa. And one single night's drinking always reduced him to this pitiful state, sick and white and trembling, and ready to swear never to drink again - quite content, in fact, not to drink for a month at least.

Rose paid no attention to his moaning and whimpering. She flung one look of scorn at him and then poured the last bottle of the case overside. She went forward and dragged the second case of gin out from among the boxes of stores. She took Allnutt's favourite screwdriver and began to prise the case open, with vicious wrenches of her powerful wrist. As the deal came away from the nails with a splintering crash, Allnutt rolled over to look at her again. With infinite trouble he got himself into a sitting position, with his hands at his temples, which felt as if they were being battered with white-hot hammers. He looked at her quite uncomprehending with his aching eyes.

"Coo Jesus!" he said, pitifully.

Rose wasted neither time nor sympathy on him; she went calmly on pouring gin overside. Allnutt got to his knees with his arms on the bench. At the second attempt he got his knees up on the bench, with his body hanging overside. Rose thought he would fall in, but she did not care. He leaned over the gurgling brown water and drank feverishly. Then he slumped back on to the bench and promptly brought up all the water he had drunk, but he felt better, all the same. The light did not hurt his eyes now.

— C.S. Forester, *The African Queen*, 1935

SLOW FADE on Rose as first daylight begins to appear.

EXT. RIVER AND THE AFRICAN QUEEN - MEDIUM CLOSE SHOT - ALLNUTT

He is prostrate beside the engine in early morning sunlight. Except that his eyes are closed, he looks as if he had been dead for about a day.

O.s., the HARSH SCRAPING of broken glass against wood and the happy shouts of early birds; also the quiet gurgling of river water.

For a few seconds, these sounds don't even register. Then they reach into him and he winces profoundly. (NOTE: Suddenly and painfully exaggerate all SOUNDS.) His dry mouth works a little. His eyelids twitch. The eyes open - and shut fast; light is painful to him.

O.s., the SOUND of a small avalanche of broken glass being thrown overside and hitting the water.

Rose's hand reaches down past the far side of his head and picks up an empty bottle and an almost empty bottle, and withdraws from SHOT. Allnutt registers vague awareness that someone is near, but doesn't open his eyes.

O.s., again painfully exaggerated, the SOUND of the gin case being DRAGGED along the deck. His eyes still shut, Allnutt suffers intense pain. He opens his eyes, squeezes them tight shut (which hurts him badly), opens them again, and gazes up past CAMERA in listless, uncomprehending horror.

ROSE - (FROM HIS VIEWPOINT)

She is in painfully bright, early sunlight, and she is wearing white. She has lifted the bottles and the case to the bench beside her. She kneels on the bench, aloof to the CAMERA. She tosses the empty bottle astern. She is on the verge of disposing of the gin in the nearly-empty bottle; on second thought she sniffs at it with mistrustful curiosity; her reaction indicates disgust with the smell, with Drink, and with Allnutt. She turns the bottle upside down and lets the contents pour overside into the river, and tosses the bottle contemptuously astern.

ALLNUTT - (SAME ANGLE AS BEFORE) - A LITTLE CLOSER

His eyes are bloodshot and are swimming with tears induced by the light. He doesn't quite take in what he sees.

ALLNUTT (a whimpering moan, pure misery; not for what he sees) Oh...Oh...!

Allnutt shuts his eyes. O.s., the GLUG-GLUG-GLUGGING of a full bottle. He looks again. He begins to comprehend and what he sees is, to him, terrible and almost unbelievable.

ALLNUTT (with deeper feeling but quietly; reacting now to what he sees) Oh...!

O.s., the SOUND of another flung bottle hitting the water, and of another being opened. Allnutt, using all his strength, manages to lift his head from the floor. The effort is so exhausting and the pain so excruciating that he just lets it fall; the bang is even more agonizing. He licks his dry lips with his dry tongue and tries speaking.

ALLNUTT (in a voice like a crow) Miss.

ROSE - (FROM HIS VIEWPOINT)
She is emptying gin and pays him no attention.

ALLNUTT'S VOICE (o.s.) *Miss?*
She pays him no attention except to turn the inverted bottle to absolute vertical.

ALLNUTT - (AS BEFORE) - A LITTLE CLOSER

ALLNUTT Have pity, Miss! (pause; SOUND of "glug-glug" o.s.) Miss? ("glug-glug") Oh, Miss, you don't know what you're doin'...I'll perish without a hair o' the dog.

SOUND, o.s., of bottle hitting water.

ALLNUTT (continuing) Ain't your property, Miss.

SOUND, o.s., of a new bottle being opened. CAMERA CREEPS CLOSER on Allnutt, whose eyes become those of a man in hell who knows, now, that his sentence is official, and permanent. With terrible effort, he lifts his head and shoulders.

MEDIUM CLOSE SHOT - ROSE - (NEUTRAL ANGLE) - NORMAL EXPOSURE

She is emptying gin. She hears the SOUNDS of Allnutt's moving o.s. Her hard face hardens still more. She glances towards him, continuing to pour.

MEDIUM SHOT - ALLNUTT - (FROM HER VIEW-POINT)

He is with great pain and effort getting himself to his knees and his arms onto the side bench. It may seem for a moment that he is going to try to come at Rose and make a struggle for it, but no: he now gets his knees to the bench and hangs his body far out over the gunwale and drinks ravenously of the muddy water. He overhangs so far that he is in clear danger of falling in.

ROSE - (SAME ANGLE AS BEFORE) - A LITTLE CLOSER

She is watching him. SOUNDS, o.s., of the gin emptying, and of his drinking. She is aware he may fall in and she doesn't care.

ALLNUTT - (AS BEFORE)

He finishes drinking and tremulously pulls himself back, and turns, and collapses into a sitting position on the bench.

ROSE - (AS BEFORE)

She is opening another bottle and casually watching him, and as casually looking away. She is pitiless, vengeful, contemptuous, and disgusted.

ALLNUTT - MEDIUM CLOSE SHOT - (NEUTRAL ANGLE)

His head hangs between his knees; his hands hang ape-like beside his ankles. After a little he is able to lift his head. He props his temples between his hands and his elbows on his knees. He is so weak that one elbow slips, letting his head fall with a nasty jolt and a whimper of anguish. He sets himself more carefully solid and gazes ahead of him at the floor.

ALLNUTT Oh...!

ROSE - (AS BEFORE)

She ignores him completely; she lays the flap back from some canned meat.

ALLNUTT - (AS BEFORE)

He gets out and fumblingly lights a cigarette; his hands are shaky. He takes a deep drag and it gives him a dreadful fit of coughing. He glances toward her piteously.

ROSE - (AS BEFORE)

She is slicing bread; she ignores him. His coughing is loud, o.s.

ALLNUTT - (AS BEFORE)

Recovered from his spasms, he timidly tries a lighter drag. This time he can taste it. It tastes foul. He puts it out, carefully, for later use, takes one look at it, and disconsolately tosses it overside. He looks again towards Rose. He looks away again. He sighs deeply and buries his face in his hands.

O.s., their SOUND abnormally sharp, the birds are singing like mad.

— James Agee, Screenplay for *The African Queen,* based on the novel by C.S. Forester, 1950

Part II

Serious Hangovers

"If the headache preceded the intoxication,
alcoholism would be a virtue."

– Samuel Butler

How often he had been dumbfounded — at first incredulous, then contemptuous — to hear someone say, after a night of drinking, "God, take it away, I don't want to smell it, I don't want to see it even, take it out of my sight!" — this at the very moment when he wanted and needed it most. Clearly it was the difference between the alcoholic and the non-.

— Charles Jackson, *The Lost Weekend*, 1944

Debussy's chamber music for harp and wind instruments got Banks back to Gratly safely and sane via the slow back roads. He had thought of stopping in at Harkside on his way to see how Annie was doing, but decided against it. He didn't want her to see him until he had at least managed a change of clothes. The ones he was wearing still stank of smoke and stale beer.

His head ached, despite the Paracetamol he had downed at Ken's flat that morning, and his mouth tasted like the bottom of a birdcage. When he had awoken and looked around Ken's living room, he had groaned at the detritus of a wild and foolish night: an empty bottle of Glenmorangie on the coffee-table, alongside an empty bottle of claret and an overflowing ashtray. He didn't think the whisky bottle had been full when they got into it, but even a fifteen-year-old would have had more sense than to mix beer, wine and whisky that way.

Still, he had enjoyed what he remembered of their rambling talk about women, marriage, divorce, sex and loneliness. And there was wonderful music. Ken was an aficionado of female jazz singers — a vinyl freak, too — and the LP sleeves scattered over the floor attested to this: Ella Fitzgerald, June Christy, Helen Forrest, Anita O'Day, Keely Smith, Peggy Lee.

The last thing Banks remembered was drifting off to late-period Billie Holiday singing "Ill Wind," her smoked-honey voice beautifully mingled with Ben Webster's tenor saxophone. Then came oblivion.

He groaned and rubbed his stubbly face. All the hangover cliches ran through his mind, one after another: You're getting too old for this sort of thing; Time you grew up; and I'll never touch another drop as long as I live. It was a familiar litany of guilt and self-disgust.

— Peter Robinson, *In a Dry Season*, 1999

The rain kept up all weekend. It was lashing the window when I opened my eyes around noon Friday, but it must have been the phone that woke me. I sat on the edge of the bed and decided not to answer it, and after a few more rings it quit.

My head ached fiercely and my gut felt like it had taken somebody's best shot. I lay down again, got up quickly when the room started to spin. In the bathroom I washed down a couple of aspirin with a half-glass of water, but they came right back up again.

I remembered the bottle Billie had pressed on me. I looked around for it and finally found it in the flight bag. I couldn't remember putting it back after the last drink of the night, but then there are other things I couldn't recall either, like most of the walk home from his apartment. That sort of miniblackout didn't bother me much. When you drove cross-country you didn't remember every billboard, every mile of highway. Why bother recalling every minute of your life?

The bottle was a third gone, and that surprised me. I could recall having had one drink with Billie while we listened to the record, then a short one before I turned the lights out. I didn't want one now, but there are the ones you want and the ones you need, and this came under the latter heading. I poured a short shot into the water glass and shuddered when I swallowed it. It didn't stay down either, but it fixed things so the next one did. And then I could swallow another couple of aspirins with another half-glass of water, and this time they stayed swallowed.

If I'd been drunk when I was born...

I stayed right there in my room. The weather gave me every reason to remain where I was, but I didn't really need an excuse. I had the sort of hangover I knew enough to treat with respect. If I'd ever felt that bad without having drunk the night before, I'd have gone straight to a hospital. As it was, I stayed put and treated myself like a man with an illness, which in retrospect would seem to have been more than a metaphor.

— Lawrence Block, *When the Sacred Gin Mill Closes*, 1986

Cully could feel the onset of a Benny hangover — a squirmy, irritable feeling. He had started into the sorry-he-had-taken-it, never-again stage. Next, depressed and jittery, he'd be looking for a scapegoat, itching for a fight.

— Frank Elli, *The Riot*, 1966

After I knew, I wanted one thing in life: I wanted Jay to love me more than he loved booze. I wanted him to look at his bottle of gin and say something like, "Oh, this bugs you? It's gone." Then toss it over his shoulder like a handful of salt. I can barely remember what I wanted before I knew. I think I wanted to be a great teacher, to inspire my athletes (or "student-athletes," as I was contractually bound to call them) to do better than they needed to. I wanted to send them off to the NFL and the major and minor leagues and their assistant coaching positions with something in their brains besides curveballs and zone defenses.

After I knew, in the second year of our marriage, I stopped drinking with Jay. I even stopped cooking with wine. I went a whole winter without making my favorite shiitake mushroom cream sauce because the mushrooms need to be soaked in one and a third cups medium-dry white wine. I tried once making it without the wine, but it wasn't the same sauce.

Shortly after our third anniversary, I stopped making my hangover soup, my top-secret, garlic-laden recipe capable of curing the most vicious hangover. I let my husband suffer, let him feel his brain was a shrunken, dried thing rattling in his skull.

In the fourth year of our marriage I took up running, thinking I could outrace my anger at Jay for being a drunk, at myself for having married a drunk, at all the various things in Texas that seemed to support drunkenness, like the billboard near the turnoff to our house that read from here to there is too far without a six-pack. On a bad night I lobbed a rock at the billboard, but it didn't even make a mark.

Near the beginning of the fifth year I stopped listening to Jay's radio show, Revel Without a Pause, broadcast six nights a week from KXAL. Jay always took a small cooler of beer to work. He always took some pot and his little metal bat (I know these words, bat, bong, kif, although I wouldn't mind forgetting them). On certain nights he encouraged his listeners to call in with their personal hangover remedies, which he carefully recorded in a black spiral notebook. He had ambitions of compiling the cures into a book, which he planned to call *How to Get the Hangover Over*. I stopped listening because I could tell from Jay's voice and his song list exactly what substances, and in what quantities, he'd ingested. Straight-up jazz meant three beers and half a joint. Coltrane's weirder stuff meant the rest of the joint. Grateful Dead meant he'd finished the six-pack. Billie Holiday meant gin.

— Louise Redd, *Hangover Soup*, 1999

The Consul, an inconceivable anguish of horripilating hangover thunderclapping about his skull, and accompanied by a protective screen of demons gnattering in his ears, became aware that in the horrid event of his being observed by his neighbours it could hardly be supposed he was just sauntering down his garden with some innocent horticultural object in mind. Nor even that he was sauntering. The Consul, who had waked a moment or two ago on the porch and everything almost immediately, was almost running. He was also lurching. In vain he tried to check himself, plunging his hands, with an extraordinary attempt at nonchalance, in which he hoped might appear more than a hint of consular majesty, deeper into the sweat-soaked pockets of his dress trousers. And now, rheumatisms discarded, he really was running...Might he not, then, be reasonably suspected of a more dramatic purpose, of having assumed, for instance, the impatient buskin of a William Blackstone leaving the Puritans to dwell among the Indians, or the desperate mien of his friend Wilson when he so magnificently abandoned the University Expedition to disappear, likewise in a pair of dress trousers, into the jungles of darkest Oceania, never to return? Not very reasonably. For one thing, if he continued much farther in this present direction towards the bottom of his garden any such visioned escape into the unknown must shortly be arrested by what was, for him, an unscalable wire fence. "Do not be so foolish as to imagine you have no object, however. We warned you, we told you so, but now that in spite of all our pleas you have got yourself into this deplorable —" He recognized the tone of one of his familiars, faint among the other voices as he crashed on through the metamorphoses of dying and reborn hallucinations, like a man who does not know he has been shot from behind. "— condition," the voice went on severely, "you have to do something about it. Therefore we are leading you towards the accomplishment of this something." "I'm not going to drink," the Consul said, halting suddenly. "Or am I? Not mescal anyway." "Of course not, the bottle's just there, behind that bush. Pick it up." "I can't," he objected — "That's right, just take one drink, just the necessary, the therapeutic drink: perhaps two drinks." "God," the Consul said. "Ah. Good. God. Christ." "Then you can say it doesn't count." "It doesn't. It isn't mescal." "Of course not, it's tequila. You might have another." "Thanks, I will." The Consul palsiedly readjusted the bottle to his lips. "Bliss. Jesus. Sanctuary...Horror," he added. "— Stop. Put that bottle down, Geoffrey Firmin, what are you doing to your-self?" another voice said in his ear so loudly he turned round. On the path before him a little snake he had thought a twig was rustling off into the bushes and he watched it a moment through his dark glasses, fas-cinated. It was a real snake all right. Not that he was much bothered by anything so simple as snakes, he reflected with a degree of pride, gazing straight into the eyes of a dog. It was a pariah dog and disturbingly familiar. "*Perro*," he repeated, as it still stood there — but had not this incident occurred, was it not now, as it were, occurring an hour or two ago, he thought in a flash. Strange. He dropped the bottle which was of white corrugated glass — Tequila Añejo de Jalisco, it said on the label — out of sight into the undergrowth, looking about him. All seemed normal again. Anyway, both snake and dog had gone. And the voices had ceased...

— Malcolm Lowry, *Under the Volcano*, 1947

Hungover But Still Working

"The test of a man is one who can work through a hangover."

— Ernest Hemingway

"I never played drunk.
Hungover, yes, but never drunk."

— Hack Wilson, Member of the Major League
Baseball Hall of Fame and outfielder for the
New York Giants, Chicago Cubs, Brooklyn
Dodgers, and Philadelphia Phillies

Harry was sick the next morning but dragged himself from the house to his office. His entire body was twitching and Harry forced down a few beers to straighten himself out before the men came. He got a couple of glasses down and half a dozen aspirin, his headache slowly leaving and the turmoil in his stomach subsiding, yet he still felt a tension, an apprehension, and he cursed the bars for not being open yet so he could get a shot and get rid of his hangover. When the men started coming, a little before 8, their joking and laughter, as they grabbed signs and had their books stamped, annoyed Harry. When all the signs had been distributed and fresh coffee made, Harry went to the bar for a couple of fast shots and came back convinced he felt better. When he got back to the office he turned the radio on and sat behind his desk drinking beer and joking with the men. When one of the officials called Harry told him he had bought a radio for the office, figured the men'd like a little music or maybe hear a ballgame when they come off the line, and the official told him to send a bill to the union and he would be reimbursed. Harry hung up the phone and sat back in his chair feeling very official and important; and although the morning passed slowly for Harry until he got over his hangover, the afternoon passed rapidly, especially after his phone conversation (strike headquarters, local 392, Black Brother talkin) with the union official.

— Hubert Selby Jr., *Last Exit to Brooklyn*, 1964

He had shaken hands with an American tycoon who was not a tycoon, and commiserated with him about his sick wife who was not sick and probably not his wife.

He was on his way to keep a rendezvous with an author who was not an author but was seeking martyrdom in a city where martyrdom could be had free across the counter, whether or not you happened to stand in line for it.

He was scared numb and had a hangover for the fourth day running.

He was a citizen of Leningrad at last.

— John le Carré, *The Russia House*, 1989

It must have been near nine the next morning when Sadie beat on my door and I came swimming and swaying up from the bottom of a muddy sleep, like a piece of sogged driftwood stirred up from the bottom of a pond. I made the door and stuck my head out.

"Listen," she said without any build-up of civilities, "Duffy's going out to the fair grounds, and I'll ride with him. He's got a lot of big-shotting to do out there. He wanted to get the sap out pretty early, too, to mingle with the common herd, but I told him he wasn't feeling too good. That he'd be out a little later."

"O.K.," I said, "I'm not paid for it, but I'll try to deliver him."

"I don't care whether he ever gets there," she said. "It won't be skin off my nose."

"I'll try to get him there anyway."

"Suit yourself," she said, and walked off down the hall, twitching the seersucker.

I looked out the window and saw that it was going to be another day, and shaved, and dressed, and went down to get a cup of coffee. Then I went to my room, and knocked. There was some kind of a sound inside, like an oboe blatting once deep inside a barrel of feathers. So I went in. I had left the door unlocked the night before.

It was after ten by that time.

Willie was on the bed. In the same place, the coat still wadded up under his armpits, his hands still crossed on his chest, his face pale and pure. I went over to the bed. His head didn't turn, but his eyes swung toward me with a motion that made you think you could hear them creak in the sockets.

"Good morning," I said.

He opened his mouth a little way and his tongue crept out and explored his lips carefully, wetting them. Then he grinned weakly as though he were experimenting to see if anything would crack. Nothing happened, so he whispered, "I reckon I was drunk last night?"

"That's the name it goes by," I said.

"It's the first time," he said. "I never got drunk before. I never even tasted it but once before."

"I know. Lucy doesn't favour drinking."

"I reckon she'll understand though when I tell her," he said. "She'll see how it was I came to do it." Then he sank into meditation.

"How do you feel?"

"I feel all right," he said, and pried himself up to a sitting posture, swinging his feet to the floor. He sat there with his sock-feet on the floor, taking stock of the internal stresses and strains. "Yeah," he concluded, "I feel all right."

"Are you going to the barbecue?"

He looked up at me with a laborious motion of the head and an expression of question on his face as though I were the one who was supposed to answer. "What made you ask that?" he demanded.

"Well, a lot's been happening."

"Yeah," he said. "I'm going."

"Duffy and Sadie have already gone. Duffy wants you to come on out and mingle with the common herd."

"All right," he said. Then, with his eyes fixed on an imaginary spot on the floor about ten feet from his toes, he stuck his tongue out again and began to caress his lips. "I'm thirsty," he said.

"You are dehydrated," I said. "The result of alcohol taken in excess. But that is the only way to take it. It is the only way to do a man any good."

But he wasn't listening. He had pulled himself up and padded off into the bathroom.

I could hear the slosh of water and the gulping and inhaling. He must have been drinking out of the faucet. After about a minute that sound stopped. There wasn't any sound at all for a spell. Then there was a new one. Then the agony was over.

He appeared at the bathroom door, braced against the doorjamb, staring at me with a face of sad reproach bedewed with the glitter of cold sweat.

"You needn't look at me like that," I said, "the likker was all right."

"I puked," he said wistfully.

"Well, you didn't invent it. Besides, now you'll be able to eat a great big, hot, juicy, high-powered slab of barbecued hog meat."

He didn't seem to think that that was very funny. And neither did I. But he didn't seem to think it was especially unfunny, either. He just hung on the doorjamb looking at me like a deaf and dumb stranger. Then he retired again into the bathroom.

"I'll order you a pot of coffee," I yelled in to him. "It'll fix you right up."

But it didn't. He took it, but it didn't even take time to make itself at home.

Then he lay down for a while. I put a cold towel on his forehead and he closed his eyes. He laid his hands on his breast, and the freckles on his face looked like rust spots on a polished cadaver.

About eleven-fifteen the desk called up to say that a car and two gentlemen were waiting to drive Mr. Stark to the fairgrounds. I put my hand over the receiver, and looked over at Willie. His eyes had come open and were fixed on the ceiling.

"What the hell do you want to go to that barbecue for?" I said. "I'm going to tell 'em to his tail."

"I'm going to the barbecue," he announced from the spirit world, his eyes still fixed on the ceiling.

So I went down to the lobby to stall off two of the local semi-leading citizens who'd even agree to ride in the gubernatorial hearse to get their names in the paper. I stalled them. I said Mr. Stark was slightly indisposed, and I would drive him out in about an hour.

At twelve o'clock I tried the coffee treatment again. It didn't work. Or rather, it worked wrong. Duffy called up from out at the fairgrounds and wanted to know what the hell. I told him he'd better go on and distribute the loaves and fishes and pray God for Willie to arrive by two o'clock.

"What's the matter?" demanded Duffy.

"Boy," I said, "the longer you don't know the happier you'll be," and hung up the phone.

Along toward one, after Willie had made another effort to recuperate with coffee and had failed, I said, "Look here, Willie, what you going out there for? Why don't you stay here? Send word you are sick and spare yourself some grief. Then, later on, if — "

"No," he said, and pushed himself up to a sitting position on the side of the bed. His face had a high and pure and transparent look like a martyr's face just before he steps into the flame.

"Well," I said, without enthusiasm, "if you are hell-bent, you got one more chance."

"More coffee?" he asked.

"No," I said, and unstrapped my suitcase and got out the second bottle. I poured some in a tumbler and took it to him. "According to the old folks," I said, "the best way is to put two shots of absinthe on a little cracked ice and float on a shot of rye. But we can't be fancy. Not with Prohibition."

He got it down. There was a harrowing moment, then I drew a sigh of relief. In ten minutes I repeated the dose. Then I told him to get undressed while I ran a tub of cold water. While he was in the tub I called down for the desk to get us a car. Then I went to Willie's room to get some clean clothes and his other suit.

He managed to get dressed, taking time out now and then for me to give him a treatment.

He got dressed and then sat on the edge of the bed wearing a big label marked *Handle with Care – This End Up – Fragile*. But I got him down to the car.

Then I had to go back up and get a copy of his speech, which he'd left in his top bureau drawer. He might need it, he said after I got back. He might not be able to remember very well, and might have to read it.

"All about Peter Rabbit and Wallie Woodchuck," I said, but he wasn't attending.

He lay back and closed his eyes while the tumbril bumped over the gravel toward the fairgrounds.

I looked up the road and saw the flivvers and wagons and buggies ranked on the outskirts of a grove, and the fair buildings, and an American flag draped around a staff against the blue sky. Then, above the sound of our coffee-grinder, I caught the strains of music. Duffy was soothing the digestion of the multitude.

Willie put out his hand and laid it on the flask. "Gimme that thing," he said.

"Go easy," I said, "you aren't used to this stuff. You already —"

But he had it to his mouth by that time and the sound of it gargling down would have drowned the sound of my words even if I had kept on wasting them.

When he handed the thing back to me, there wasn't enough in it to make it worth my while putting it in my pocket. What collected in one corner when I tilted it wouldn't make even a drink for a high-school girl. "You sure you don't want to finish it?" I asked in mock politeness.

He shook his head in a dazed sort of way, said, "No, thanks," and then shivered like a man with a hard chill.

So I took what was left, and threw the empty pint bottle out of the window.

"Drive in as close as you can," I told the boy at the wheel.

He got in pretty close, and I got out and gave Willie a hand, and paid the kid off. Then Willie and I drifted slowly over the brown and trodden grass toward a platform, while the crowd about us was as nothing and Willie's eyes were on far horizons and the band played "Casey Jones."

I left Willie in the lee of the platform, standing all alone in a space of brown grass in a strange country with a dream on his face and the sun beating down on him.

I found Duffy, and said, "I'm ready to make delivery, but I want a receipt."

"What's the matter with him?" Duffy wanted to know. "The bastard doesn't drink. Is he drunk?"

"He never touches the stuff," I said. "It's just he's been on the road to Damascus and he saw a great light and he's got the blind staggers."

"What's the matter with him?"

"You ought to read the Good Book more," I told Duffy, and led him to the candidate. It was a touching reunion. So I melted into the throng.

There was quite a crowd, for the scent of burning meat on the air will do wonders. The folks were beginning to collect around in front of the platform, and climb up in the grandstand. The local band was standing over to one side of the platform, now working over "Hail, Hail, the Gang's All Here." On the platform were the two local boys who didn't have any political future, who had come to the hotel that morning, and another fellow who was by my guess a preacher to offer up a prayer, and Duffy. And there was Willie, sweating slow. They sat in a row of chairs across the back of the platform, in front of the bunting-draped backdrop, and behind a bunting-draped table on which was a big pitcher of water and a couple of glasses.

One of the local boys got up first and addressed his friends and neighbours and introduced the preacher who addressed God-Almighty with his gaunt raw-boned face lifted up above the blue serge and his eyes squinched into the blazing light. Then the first local boy got up and worked around to introducing the second local boy. It looked for a while as though the second local boy was the boy with the button after all, for he was, apparently, built for endurance and not speed, but it turned out that he didn't really have the button any more than the first local boy or the preacher or God-Almighty. It just took him longer to admit that he didn't have it and to put the finger on Willie.

Then Willie stood all alone by the table, saying, "My friends," and turning his alabaster face precariously from one side to the other, and fumbling in the right side pocket of his coat to fish out the speech.

While he was fumbling with the sheets, and looking down at them with a slightly bemused expression as though the stuff before him were in a foreign language, somebody tugged at my sleeve. There was Sadie.

"How was it?" she asked.

"Take a look and guess," I replied.

She gave a good look up to the platform, and then asked, "How'd you do it?"

"Hair of the dog."

She looked up to the platform again. "Hair, hell," she said, "he must have swallowed the dog."

I inspected Willie, who stood up there sweating and swaying and speechless, under the hot sun.

"He's on the ropes," Sadie said.

"Hell, he's been on 'em all morning," I said, "and lucky to have 'em."

She was still looking at him. It was much the way she had looked at him the night before when he lay on the bed in my room, out cold, and she stood by the side of the bed. It wasn't pity and it wasn't contempt. It was an ambiguous, speculative look. Then she said, "Maybe he was born on 'em."

She said it in a tone that seemed to imply that she had settled that subject. But she kept on looking up there at him in the same way.

The candidate could still stand, at least with one thigh propped against the table. He had begun to talk by this time, too. He had called them his friends in two or three ways and had said he was glad to be there. Now he stood there clutching the manuscript in both hands, with his head lowered like a dehorned cow beset by a couple of fierce dogs in the barnyard, while the sun beat on him and the sweat dropped. Then he took a grip on himself, and lifted his head.

— Robert Penn Warren, *All the King's Men*, 1946

I shaved, showered, tossed a couple of coffees down and called the Waldorf to see if the Argentine delegation was going out with me. Fernando answered the phone. Pepe had just gone to bed. He had left a call for four that afternoon. But Fernando wanted to go with me. He thought it would be a good idea if Toro, in his interview, said something about the growing importance of the national sports movement in Argentina. So for one hour on that bumpy local, with an off-key version of the Anvil Chorus pounding in my head, I had to hear about the growing enthusiasm for *Argentinidad*.

— Budd Schulberg, *The Harder The Fall*, 1947

The purpose of a battle climb was to lift the squadron to combat height in the minimum time. It was hard work for men and machines, the engines slogging away to win a couple of thousand feet every minute, the pilots having to hold tight formation through cloud and air pockets and a change of atmosphere equivalent to climbing the Alps in a quarter of an hour. There was no chance to relax: everything and everyone toiled flat-out. It was the Ram's favourite manoeuvre.

"Jester Leader to Red Three: close up, damn you," he ordered for the third time.

Stickwell was Red Three. His wingtip was ten feet from the Ram's wingtip. He cut the gap to five feet and concentrated grimly on holding the position. His stomach kept jumping as if someone were poking it with a pencil, and his mouth tasted stiff and sour; also his skull seemed to be pressing down on his eyeballs. He knew it was only a matter of time before he was sick.

At last the Ram looked away from him. Just you wait, Flying Officer Stickwell, the Ram said to himself. I'll teach you to get blotto. I'll spread your guts all over this sky before I'm through. He opened his transmission switch. "Jester Leader to Red Two: where the hell d'you think you're going?" he said.

Cattermole was Red Two. He had already been sick: the effect of too much pure oxygen on a system thoroughly abused by alcohol and horseriding. Oxygen was a well known hangover cure for fighter pilots but on this occasion, although it had cleared his head, it had emptied his stomach. He didn't mind being sick but the vomit had splashed onto his gloves and made them slippery. Whenever he tried to wipe them clean, he wandered out of formation. "Sorry, leader," he said, and drifted back.

— Derek Robinson, Piece of Cake, 1983

Nora and I went to the opening of *Honeymoon* at the Little Theatre that night and then to a party given by some people named Freeman or Fielding or something. I felt pretty low when she called me the next morning. She gave me a newspaper and a cup of coffee and said: "Read that."

I patiently read a paragraph or two, then put the paper down and took a sip of coffee. "Fun's fun," I said, "but right now I'd swap you all the interviews with Mayor-elect O'Brien ever printed – and throw in the Indian picture – for a slug of whis–"

"Not that, stupid." She put a finger on the paper. "That."

INVENTOR'S SECRETARY MURDERED IN APARTMENT

JULIA WOLF'S BULLET-RIDDLED BODY FOUND; POLICE SEEK HER EMPLOYER, CLYDE WYNANT

The bullet-riddled body of Julia Wolf, thirty-two-year-old confidential secretary to Clyde Miller Wynant, well-known inventor, was discovered late yesterday afternoon in the dead woman's apartment at 411 East Fifty-fourth St. by Mrs. Christian Jorgensen, divorced wife of the inventor, who had gone there in an attempt to learn her former husband's present address.

Mrs. Jorgensen, who returned Monday after a six-year stay in Europe, told police that she heard feeble groans when she rang the murdered woman's door-bell, whereupon she notified an elevator boy, Mervin Holly, who called Walter Meany, apartment-house superintendent. Miss Wolf was lying on the bedroom floor with four .32-calibre bullet-wounds in her chest when they entered the apartment, and died without having recovered consciousness before police and medical aid arrived.

Herbert Macauley, Wynant's attorney, told the police that he had not seen the inventor since

October. He stated that Wynant called him on the telephone yesterday and made an appointment, but failed to keep it; and disclaimed any knowledge of his client's whereabouts. Miss Wolf, Macauley stated, had been in the inventor's employ for the past eight years. The attorney said he knew nothing about the dead woman's family or private affairs and could throw no light on her murder.

The bullet-wounds could not have been self-inflicted, according to...

The rest of it was the usual police department hand-out.

"Do you suppose he killed her?" Nora asked when I put the paper down again.

"Wynant? I wouldn't be surprised. He's batty as hell."

"Did you know her?"

"Yes. How about a drop if something to cut the phlegm?"

"What was she like?"

"Not bad," I said. "She wasn't bad-looking and she had a lot of sense and a lot of nerve - and it took both to live with that guy."

"She lived with him?"

"Yes. I want a drink, please. That is, it was like that when I knew them."

"Why don't you have some breakfast first? Was she in love with him or was it just business?"

"I don't know. It's too early for breakfast."

When Nora opened the door to go out, the dog came in and put her front feet on the bed, her face in my face. I rubbed her head and tried to remember something Wynant had once said to me, something

about women and dogs. It was not the woman-span-
iel-walnut-tree line. I could not remember what it
was, but there seemed to be some point in trying to
remember.

Nora returned with two drinks and another question: "What's he like?"

"Tall - over six feet - and one of the thinnest men
I've ever seen. He must be about fifty now, and his
hair was almost white when I knew him. Usually
needs a haircut, ragged brindle mustache, bites his fingernails." I pushed the dog away to reach for my drink.

"Sounds lovely. What were you doing with him?"

"A fellow who'd worked for him accused him of
stealing some kind of idea or invention from him. Kelt-
erman was his name. He tried to shake Wynant down
by threatening to shoot him, bomb his house, kidnap
his children, cut his wife's throat - I don't know what
all - if he didn't come across. We never caught him -
must've scared him off. Anyway, the threats stopped
and nothing happened."

Nora stopped drinking to ask: "Did Wynant really
steal it?"

"Tch, tch, tch," I said. "This is Christmas Eve: try
to think good of your fellow man."

— Dashiell Hammett, *The Thin Man*, 1934

Corporal Everit Cudlipp, reeking and hung over, his
pounding head held together by a set of headphones,
shifted uncomfortably in his chair, doing battle in a
losing cause against flatulence. His growing paunch
had been nurtured by a daily quota of beer, and there
were sounds hissing and popping within it. No one
heard these noises, for all Cudlipp's neighbours also

had their ears enclosed in headphones. They were members of Special I, the bugging squad. The only sounds in the wiretap-monitoring room were the whirring noises of reel-to-reel recorders.

— William Deverell, *Needles*, 1979

It was Saturday night, so the people in our *bistro* were busy getting drunk, and with a free day ahead of me I was ready to join them. We all went to bed, drunk, at two in the morning, meaning to sleep till noon. At half-past five I was suddenly awakened. A night-watchman, sent from the hotel, was standing at my bedside. He stripped the clothes back and shook me roughly.

"Get up," he said. "*Tu t'es bien saoule la gueule, pas vrai?* Well, never mind that, the hotel's a man short. You've got to work today."

"Why should I work?" I protested. "This is my day off."

"Day off, nothing! The work's got to be done. Get up!"

I got up and went out, feeling as though my back were broken and my skull filled with hot cinders. I did not think that I could possibly do a day's work. And yet, after only an hour in the basement, I found that I was perfectly well. It seemed that in the heat of those cellars, as in a Turkish bath, one could sweat out almost any quantity of drink. *Plongeurs* know this, and count on it. The power of swallowing quarts of wine, and then sweating it out before it can do much damage, is one of the compensations of their life.

— George Orwell, *Down and Out in Paris and London*, 1933

And Sometimes Hungover But Not Working

Then Jonathan made one telephone call to a client who had an important picture to pick up, to say that he would be closed Tuesday and Wednesday for "reasons of family", a common excuse. He'd have to leave a sign to that effect in his door for a couple of days. Not a very important matter, Jonathan thought, since shopkeepers in town frequently closed for a few days for one reason or another. Jonathan had once seen a sign saying "closed due to hangover".

— Patricia Highsmith, *Ripley's Game*, 1974

Or sometimes working, but not hungover.

I, Friedrich Engels, supreme poet in the Bremen town-hall cellar and privileged boozer, announce and make known to all and sundry, past, present, absent and future, that you are all asses, lazy creatures, who are wasting away from disgust with your own existence, scoundrels who don't write to me, and so on, and so on. Written on our office stool at a time when we had no hangover.

— Friedrich Engels, 1839

Hangover

Music by Kim Mitchell; Lyrics by Pye Dubois
Recorded by Max Webster on their self-titled
1976 album

Tomorrow don't be here today
Take a cruise, take a holiday
Cold morning and the drums
Blue eyes in the window sun

I don't feel you but I know you're around
I can feel you cause I feel the sound
Cold morning and the drums, blue eyes in the window
    sun
Alka Seltzer, Tang and a 50
It's all over
Hangover

It's getting warmer
It's controlling my mind
It's coming closer
I'm biding my time
Double vision when the bars close down
Double vision when the bars close down

My legs are weak
Her arms are strong
The door is open
The stairs are steep
The room is near
Yet oh so far
The lights are round
But so are the stars

I don't feel you but I know you're around
I can feel you cause I feel the sound
Cold morning and the drums, blue eyes in the window
    sun
Alka Seltzer, Tang and a 50
It's all over
You got a hangover
I got a hangover

You Were Perfectly Fine
by Dorothy Parker

The pale young man eased himself carefully into the low chair, and rolled his head to the side, so that the cool chintz comforted his cheek and temple.

"Oh, dear," he said, "Oh, dear, oh, dear, oh, dear. Oh."

The clear-eyed girl, sitting light and erect on the couch, smiled brightly at him.

"Not feeling so well today?" she said.

"Oh, I'm great," he said. "Corking, I am. Know what time I got up? Four o'clock this afternoon, sharp. I kept trying to make it, and every time I took my head off the pillow, it would roll under the bed. This isn't my head I've got on now. I think this is something that used to belong to Walt Whitman. Oh, dear, oh, dear, oh, dear."

"Do you think maybe a drink would make you feel better?" she said.

"The hair of the mastiff that bit me?" he said. "Oh, no, thank you. Please never speak of anything like that again. I'm through. I'm all, all through. Look at that hand; steady as a humming-bird. Tell me, was I very terrible last night?"

"Oh, goodness," she said, "everybody was feeling pretty high. You were all right."

"Yeah," he said. "I must have been dandy. Is everybody sore at me?"

"Good heavens, no," she said. "Everyone thought you were terribly funny. Of course, Jim Pierson was a little stuffy, there, for a minute at dinner. But people sort of held him back in his chair, and got him calmed down. I don't think anybody at the other tables noticed it at all. Hardly anybody."

"He was going to sock me?" he said. "Oh, Lord. What did I do to him?"

"Why, you didn't do a thing," she said. "You were perfectly fine. But you know how silly Jim gets, when he thinks anybody is making too much fuss over Elinor."

"Was I making a pass at Elinor?" he said. "Did I do that?"

"Of course you didn't," she said. "You were only fooling, that's all. She thought you were awfully amusing. She was having a marvelous time. She only got a little tiny bit annoyed just once, when you poured the clam-juice down her back."

"My God," he said. "Clam-juice down that back. And every vertebra a little Cabot. Dear God. What'll I ever do?"

"Oh, she'll be all right," she said. "Just send her some flowers, or something. Don't worry about it. It isn't anything."

"No, I won't worry," he said. "I haven't got a care in the world. I'm sitting pretty. Oh, dear, oh, dear. Did I do any other fascinating tricks at dinner?"

"You were fine," she said. "Don't be so foolish about it. Everybody was crazy about you. The *maître d'hôtel* was a little worried because you wouldn't stop singing, but he really didn't mind. All he said was, he was afraid they'd close the place again, if there was so much noise. But he didn't care a bit, himself. I think he loved seeing you have such a good time. Oh, you were just singing away, there, for about an hour. It wasn't so terribly loud, at all."

"So I sang," he said. "That must have been a treat. I sang."

"Don't you remember?" she said. "You just sang one song after another. Everybody in the place was listening. They loved it. Only you kept insisting that you wanted to sing some song about some kind of fusiliers or other, and everybody kept shushing you, and you'd keep trying to start it again. You were wonderful. We were all trying to make you stop singing for a minute, and eat something, but you wouldn't hear of it. My, you were funny."

"Didn't I eat any dinner?" he said.

"Oh, not a thing," she said. "Every time the waiter would offer you something, you'd give it right back to him, because you said that he was your long-lost brother, changed in the cradle by a gypsy band, and that anything you had was his. You had him simply roaring at you."

"I bet I did," he said. "I bet I was comical Society's Pet, I must have been. And what happened then, after my overwhelming success with the waiter?"

"Why, nothing much," she said. "You took a sort of dislike to some old man with white hair, sitting across the room, because you didn't like his necktie and you wanted to tell him about it. But we got you out, before he got really mad."

"Oh, we got out," he said. "Did I walk?"

"Walk! Of course you did," she said. "You were absolutely all right. There was that nasty stretch of ice on the sidewalk, and you did sit down awfully hard, you poor dear. But good heavens, that might have happened to anybody."

"Oh, sure," he said. "Louisa Alcott or anybody. So I fell down on the sidewalk. That would explain what's the matter with my — Yes, I see. And then what, if you don't mind?"

"Ah, now, Peter!" she said. "You can't sit there and say you don't remember what happened after that! I did think that maybe you were just a little tight at dinner — oh, you were perfectly all right, and all that, but I did know you were feeling pretty gay. But you were so serious, from the time you fell down — I never knew you to be that way. Don't you know, how you told me I had never seen your real self before? Oh, Peter, I just couldn't bear it, if you didn't remember that lovely long ride we took together in the taxi! Please, you do remember that, don't you? I think it would simply kill me, if you didn't."

"Oh, yes," he said. "Riding in the taxi. Oh, yes, sure. Pretty long ride, hmm?"

"Round and round and round the park," she said. "Oh, and the trees were shining so in the moonlight. And you said you never knew before that you really had a soul."

"Yes," he said. "I said that. That was me."

"You said such lovely, lovely things," she said. "And I'd never known, all this time, how you had been feeling about me, and I'd never dared to let you see how I felt about you. And then last night — oh, Peter dear, I think that taxi ride was the most important thing that has ever happened to us in our lives."

"Yes," he said. "I guess it must have been."

"And we're going to be so happy," she said. "Oh, I just want to tell everybody! But I don't know — I think maybe it would be sweeter to keep it all to ourselves."

"I think it would be," he said.

"Isn't it lovely?" she said.

"Yes," he said. "Great."

"Lovely!" she said.

"Look here," he said, "do you mind if I have a drink? I mean, just medicinally, you know. I'm off the stuff for life, so help me. But I think I feel a collapse coming on."

"Oh, I think it would do you good," she said. "You poor boy, it's a shame you feel so awful. I'll go make you a whisky and soda."

"Honestly," he said, "I don't see how you could ever want to speak to me again, after I made such a fool of myself, last night. I think I'd better go join a monastery in Tibet."

"You crazy idiot!" she said. "As if I could ever let you go away now! Stop talking like that. You were perfectly fine."

She jumped up from the couch, kissed him quickly on the forehead, and ran out of the room.

The pale young man looked after her and shook his head long and slowly, then dropped it in his damp and trembling hands.

"Oh, dear," he said. "Oh, dear, oh, dear, oh, dear."

Some Mornings of Samuel Pepys

❦

Perhaps the greatest diarist in the English language, Samuel Pepys left behind an invaluable and insightful portrait of everyday life and manners in 17ᵗʰcentury London. Nothing escaped Pepys' attention, not even hangovers. To whit, some selected entries.

9 March 1660

All night troubled in my thoughts how to order my business upon this great change with me, that I could not sleep; and being overheated with drink, I made a promise the next morning to drink no strong drink this week, for I find that it makes me sweat in bed and puts me quite out of order.

22 September 1660

To Westminster to my Lord's; and there in the house of office vomited up all my breakfast, my stomach being ill all this day by reason of last night's debauch.

2 December 1660

Lord's day. My head not very well and my body out of order by last night's drinking — which is my great folly.

3 April 1661

Up among my workmen, my head akeing all day from last night's debauch. To the office all the morning, and at noon dined with Sir W Batten and Pen, who would needs have me drink two drafts of sack to-day to cure me of last night's disease, which I thought strange but I think find it true.

24 April 1661

Waked in the morning with my head in a sad taking through the last night's drink, which I am very sorry for. So rise and went out with Mr. Creed to drink our morning draught, which he did give me in Chocolate to settle my stomach.

Part III

"Helpless as a pickled herring"

He remained silent as Jake Harp casually knocked his second shot thirty feet from the pin.

"What was that, a five-iron? A six?"

"A six," replied Jake Harp, pinching the bridge of his nose. He figured if he could just cut off circulation, it would starve the pain behind his eyeballs and make his hangover go away.

— Carl Hiaasen, *Native Tongue*, 1991

He led me up a curved iron stair to an iron-railed gallery with a riveted floor. We passed a series of iron-sheathed doors with small wire-reinforced windows. There were shouts and howls and laughter behind one of them.

"Drunk tank," Marsland said. "It's just like fiesta on a Saturday night. But oh on Sunday morning!"

— Ross MacDonald, *Meet Me at the Morgue*, 1953

"I've got your number," said Rosalie Le Grange. "There's a small million like you. Let me tell you about yourself. You're young. You've got neither family nor girl here in New York. There's nothing for you to do nights but to meet the boys. An' you begin to pour it down. The next thing you know, or don't know, you're drunk an' uncomfortable. Ain't that so?"

"Uncomfortable!" exclaimed Tommy North; "when I'm drunk? Woman, I own New York! I have an option on the Hudson Terminal and a mortgage on the Singer Building. Of course, the next morning when I'm undrunk, there's a pale Jerseyish cast over the face of things." This was the first time in his life that Tommy North had ever admitted a "hangover". He used to tell his companions that hard liquor was his beefsteak.

— Will Irwin, *The Red Button*, 1912 (Possibly the first time the word hangover, in its current meaning, was used in a work of literature.)

I was awakened by the sound of someone calling my name but I guess it must have been my imagination. I was probably still imagining things from the evening before. A glance at my wrist watch showed the time to be nearly three and I was really quite surprised. I thought it was much later.

I arose with much unsteadiness, having one of my usual hangovers. A shower and several bromo-seltzers would make me fit again, I thought, for I had to look fairly sober when I presented myself to the family for inspection.

— James Stuart Gillespie Jr., *Hangover 1936*, 1937

[They] walked off in separate directions through the chaparral to stand spraddlelegged clutching their knees and vomiting. The browsing horses jerked their heads up. It was no sound they'd ever heard before. In the gray twilight those retchings seemed to echo like the calls of some rude provisional species loosed upon that waste. Something imperfect and malformed lodged in the heart of being. A thing smirking deep in the eyes of grace itself like a gorgon in an autumn pool.

— Cormac MacCarthy, *All the Pretty Horses*, 1992

In the hangover of the morning after, a million mischievous imps bored into his brain with riveting-machines and his eyelids were swollen and heavy. The room swam about his head like a wave-pitched dory and the noise of the trolleys rattling by below was magnified to thunderstorm proportions. A nauseous feeling seized him and he felt as helpless as a pickled herring.

The nine-thirty call stirred him from his lethargy and the ringing of the phone made him vaguely realize that these were his bridal bells pealing and that it was his wedding morning.

He dragged himself out of bed and limped over to silence the instrument. After a cold shower in the bathroom and a hot towel in the barber-shop, he felt much better.

— Max Lief, *Hangover* (republished as *Wild Parties*), 1929

It was a few days later than this that the pigs came upon a case of whisky in the cellars of the farmhouse. It had been overlooked at the time when the house was first occupied. That night there came from the farmhouse the sound of loud singing, in which, to everyone's surprise, the strains of 'Beasts of England' were mixed up. At about half-past nine Napoleon, wearing an old bowler hat of Mr. Jones's, was distinctly seen to emerge from the back door, gallop rapidly round the yard and disappear indoors again. But in the morning a deep silence hung over the farmhouse. Not a pig appeared to be stirring. It was nearly nine o'clock when Squealer made his appearance, walking slowly and dejectedly, his eyes dull, his tail hanging limply behind him, and with every appearance of being seriously ill. He called the animals together and told them he had a terrible piece of news to impart. Comrade Napoleon was dying!

A cry of lamentation went up. Straw was laid down outside the doors of the farmhouse, and the animals walked on tiptoe. With tears in their eyes they asked one another what they should do if their leader were taken away from them. A rumour went round that Snowball had after all contrived to introduce poison into Napoleon's food. At eleven o'clock Squealer came out to make another announcement. As his last act upon earth, Comrade Napoleon had pronounced a solemn decree: the drinking of alcohol was to be punished by death.

By the evening, however, Napoleon appeared to be somewhat better, and by the following morning Squealer was able to tell them that he was well on the way to recovery. By the evening of that day Napoleon was back at work, and on the next day it was learned that he had instructed Whymper to purchase in Wilingdon some booklets on brewing and distilling. A week later Napoleon gave orders that the small paddock beyond the orchard, which it had previously been intended to set aside as a grazing-ground for animals who were past work, was to be ploughed up. It was given out that the pasture was exhausted and needed re-seeding: but it soon became known that Napoleon intended to sow it with barley.

About this time there occurred a strange incident which hardly anyone was able to understand. One night at about twelve o'clock there was a loud crash in the yard, and the animals rushed out of their stalls. It was a moonlit night. At the foot of the end wall of the big barn, where the Seven Commandments were written, there lay a ladder broken in two pieces. Squealer, temporarily stunned, was sprawling beside it, and near at hand there lay a lantern, a paintbrush and an overturned pot of white paint. The dogs immediately made a ring around Squealer, and escorted him back to the farmhouse as soon as he was able to walk. None of the animals could form any idea as to what this meant, except old Benjamin, who nodded his muzzle with a knowing air, and seemed to understand, but would say nothing.

But a few days later Muriel, reading over the Seven Commandments to herself, noticed that there was yet another of them which the animals had remembered wrong. They had thought that the Fifth Commandment was 'No animal shall drink alcohol', but there were two words that they had forgotten. Actually the Commandment read: 'No animal shall drink alcohol *to excess.*'

— George Orwell, *Animal Farm*, 1945

How somebody, lying in my bed, lay saying and doing all this over again, at cross purposes, in a feverish dream all night - the bed a rocking sea that was never still! How, as that somebody slowly settled down into myself, did I begin to parch, and feel as if my outer covering of skin were a hard board; my tongue the bottom of an empty kettle, furred with long service, and burning up over a slow fire; the palms of my hands, hot plates of metal which no ice could cool!

But the agony of mind, the remorse, and shame I felt, when I became conscious next day! My horror of having committed a thousand offenses I had forgotten, and which nothing could ever expiate - my recollection of that indelible look which Agnes had given me - the torturing impossibility of communicating with her, not knowing, beast that I was, how she came to be in London, or where she stayed - my disgust of the very sight of the room where the revel had been held - my racking head - the smell of smoke, the sight of glasses, the impossibility of going out, or even getting up! Oh, what a day it was.

Oh, what an evening, when I sat down by my fire to a basin of mutton broth, dimpled all over with fat, and thought I was going the way of my predecessor, and should succeed to his dismal story as well as to his chambers, and had half a mind to rush express to Dover and reveal all! What an evening, when Mrs. Crupp, coming in to take away the broth-basin, produced one kidney on a cheese-plate as the entire remains of yesterday's feast, and I was really inclined to fall upon her nankeen breast, and say, in heartfelt penitence, "Oh, Mrs. Crupp, Mrs. Crupp, never mind the broken meats! I am very miserable!" - only that I doubted, even at that pass, if Mrs. Crupp were quite the sort of woman to confide in!

— Charles Dickens, *David Copperfield*, 1850

Doc awakened very slowly and clumsily like a fat man getting out of a swimming pool. His mind broke the surface and fell back several times. There was red lipstick on his beard. He opened one eye, saw the brilliant colours of the quilt and closed his eye quickly. But after a while he looked again. His eye went past the quilt to the floor, to the broken plate in the corner, to the glasses standing on the table turned over on the floor, to the spilled wine and the books like heavy fallen butterflies. There were little bits of curled red paper all over the place and the sharp smell of fire-crackers. He could see through the kitchen door to the steak plates stacked high and the skillets deep in grease. Hundreds of cigarette butts were stamped out on the floor. And under the firecracker smell was a fine combination of wine and whiskey and perfume. His eye stopped for a moment on a little pile of hair-pins in the middle of the floor.

He rolled over slowly and supporting himself on one elbow he looked out the broken window. Can-nery Row was quiet and sunny. The boiler door was open. The door of the Palace Flophouse was closed. A man slept peacefully among the weeds in the vacant lot. The Bear Flag was shut up tight.

Doc got up and went into the kitchen and lighted the gas water heater on his way to the toilet. Then he came back and sat on the edge of his bed and worked his toes together while he surveyed the wreckage. From up the hill he could hear the church bells ringing. When the gas heater began rumbling he went back to the bathroom and took a shower and he put on blue jeans and a flannel shirt. Lee Chong was closed but he saw who was at the door and opened it. He went to the refrigerator and brought out a quart of beer without being asked. Doc paid him.

"Good time?" Lee asked. His brown eyes were a little inflamed in their pouches.

"Good time!" said Doc and he went back to the laboratory with his cold beer. He made a peanut butter sandwich to eat with his beer. It was very quiet in the street.

— John Steinbeck, *Cannery Row*, 1945

Tony Wilde woke with a throbbing head and cold feet. In the early morning half light he looked, with one rheumy eye opened, towards Pansy Loke's tousled hair topping a cocoon of blankets next to him. A shaking hand reached to explore her body but a wave of nausea killed the urge. "Nothing's bloody right these days," he mumbled as he rolled out of bed. Struggling into an ancient dressing gown he staggered off first to the bathroom and then the kitchen to remedy the effect of little sleep and many farewell parties, particularly the one he and Pansy left a few hours earlier.

"Ah Tong," he croaked at the kitchen door and slumped into an easy chair in the living room while his houseboy filled a prescription of Alka Seltzer and black coffee with brandy.

— Leonard Rayner, *Dragon's Tale*, 1989

Dundridge woke in a lay-by on the London road. He had a splitting headache, he was extremely cold and the gear lever was sticking into his ribs. He sat up, untangled his legs from under the steering wheel and wondered where the hell he was, how he had got there and what the devil had happened. He had an extremely clear memory of the party at the Golf Club. He could remember talking to Miss Boles on the terrace. He could even recall walking back to his car with her. After that nothing.

He got out of the car to try to get the circulation moving in his legs and discovered that his trousers were undone. He did them up hurriedly and reached up automatically to tighten the knot in his tie to hide his embarrassment only to find that he wasn't wearing a tie. He felt his open shirt collar and the vest underneath. It was on back to front. He pulled the vest out a bit and looked down at the label. St. Michael Combed Cotton it said. It was definitely on back to front. Now he came to think of it, his Y-fronts felt peculiar too. He took a step forward and tripped over a shoelace. His shoes were untied. Dundridge staggered against the car, seriously alarmed. He was in the middle of nowhere at...He looked at his watch. At six a.m., with his shoes untied, his vest and pants on back to front, and his trousers undone, and all he could remember was getting into the car with a girl with almond eyes and lovely legs.

And suddenly Dundridge had a horrid picture of the night's events. Perhaps he had raped the girl. A sudden brainstorm. That would explain the headache. The years of self-indulgence with his composite woman had come home to roost. He had gone mad and raped Miss Boles, possibly killed her. He looked down at his hands. At least there wasn't any blood on them. He could have strangled her. There was always that possibility. There were any number of awful possibilities. Dundridge bent over painfully and did up his shoes and then, having looked in the ditch to make sure that there was no body there, he got back into the car and wondered what to do. There was obviously no point in sitting in the lay-by. Dundridge started the car and drove on until he came to a signpost which told him he was going towards London. He turned the car round and drove back to Wotford, parked in the yard of the Handyman Arms and went quietly up to his room. He was in bed when the girl brought him his tea.

"What time is it?" he asked sleepily. The girl looked at him with a nasty smile.

"You ought to know," she said, "you've only just come in. I saw you sneaking up the stairs. Been having a night on the tiles, have you?"

She put the tray down and went out, leaving Dundridge cursing himself for a fool. He drank some tea and felt worse. There was no point in doing anything until he felt better. He turned on his side and went to sleep.

— Tom Sharpe, *Blott on the Landscape*, 1975

It was the best of nationally advertised and quantitatively produced alarm-clocks, with all the modern attachments, including cathedral chime, intermittent alarm, and a phosphorescent dial. Babbitt was proud of being awakened by such a rich device. Socially it was almost as creditable as buying expensive cord tires.

He sulkily admitted now that there was no more escape, but he lay and detested the grind of the real-estate business, and disliked his family, and disliked himself for disliking them. The evening before, he had played poker at Virgil Gunch's till midnight, and after such holidays he was irritable before breakfast. It may have been the tremendous home-brewed beer of the prohibition era and the cigars to which that beer enticed him; it may have been resentment of return from this fine, bold man-world to a restricted region of wives and stenographers, and of suggestions not to smoke too much.

From the bedroom beside the sleeping-porch, his wife's detestably cheerful "Time to get up, Georgie-boy," and the itchy sound, the brisk and scratchy sound, of combing hairs out of a stiff brush.

He grunted; he dragged his thick legs, in baby-blue pajamas, from under the khaki blanket; he sat on the edge of the cot, running his fingers through his wild hair, while his plump feet mechanically felt for his slippers. He looked regretfully at the blanket — forever a suggestion to him of freedom and heroism. He had bought it for a camping trip which had never come off. It symbolized gorgeous loafing, gorgeous cursing, virile flannel shirts.

He creaked to his feet, groaning at the waves of pain which passed behind his eyeballs. Though he waited for their scorching recurrence, he looked blurrily out at the yard. It delighted him, as always; it was the neat yard of a successful business man of Zenith, that is, it was perfection, and made him also perfect. He regarded the corrugated iron garage. For the three-hundred-and-sixty-fifth time in a year he reflected, "No class to that tin shack. Have to build me a frame garage. But by golly it's the only thing on the place that isn't up-to-date!" While he stared he thought of a community garage for his acreage development, Glen Oriole. He stopped puffing and jiggling. His arms were akimbo. His petulant, sleep-swollen face was set in harder lines. He suddenly seemed capable, an official, a man to contrive, to direct, to get things done.

On the vigor of his idea he was carried down the hard, clean, unused-looking hall into the bathroom.

Though the house was not large it had, like all houses on Floral Heights, an altogether royal bathroom of porcelain and glazed tile and metal sleek as silver. The towel-rack was a rod of clear glass set in nickel. The tub was long enough for a Prussian Guard, and above the set bowl was a sensational exhibit of tooth-brush holder, shaving-brush holder, soap-dish, sponge-dish, and medicine-cabinet, so glittering and so ingenious that they resembled an electrical instrument-board. But the Babbitt whose god was Modern Appliances was not pleased. The air of the bathroom was thick with the smell of a heathen toothpaste. "Verona been at it again! 'Stead of sticking to Lilidol, like I've re-peat-ed-ly asked her, she's gone and gotten some confounded stinkum stuff that makes you sick!"

The bath-mat was wrinkled and the floor was wet. (His daughter Verona eccentrically took baths in the morning, now and then.) He slipped on the mat, and slid against the tub. He said, "Damn!" Furiously he snatched up his tube of shaving-cream, furiously he lathered, with a belligerent slapping of the unctuous brush, furiously he raked his plump cheeks with a safety-razor. It pulled. The blade was dull. He said, "Damn - oh - oh - damn it!"

He hunted through the medicine-cabinet for a packet of new razor-blades (reflecting, as invariably, "Be cheaper to buy one of these dinguses and strop your own blades,") and when he discovered the packet, behind the round box of bicarbonate of soda, he thought ill of his wife for putting it there and very well of himself for not saying "Damn." But he did say it, immediately afterward, when with wet and soap-slippery fingers he tried to remove the horrible little envelope and crisp clinging oiled paper from the new blade.

Then there was the problem, oft-pondered, never solved, of what to do with the old blade, which might imperil the fingers of his young. As usual, he tossed it on top of the medicine-cabinet, with a mental note that some day he must remove the fifty or sixty other blades that were also temporarily, piled up there. He finished his shaving in a growing testiness increased by his spinning headache and by the emptiness in his stomach. When he was done, his round face smooth and streamy and his eyes stinging from soapy water, he reached for a towel. The family towels were wet, wet and clammy and vile, all of them wet, he found, as he blindly snatched them - his own face-towel, his wife's, Verona's, Ted's, Tinka's, and the lone bath towel with the huge welt of initial. Then George F. Babbitt did a dismaying thing. He wiped his face on the guest-towel! It was a pansy-embroidered trifle which always hung there to indicate that the Babbitts were in the best Floral Heights society. No one had ever used it. No guest had ever dared to. Guests secretively took a corner of the nearest regular towel.

He was raging, "By golly, here they go and use up all the towels, every doggone one of 'em, and they use 'em and get 'em all wet and sopping, and never put out a dry one for me - of course, I'm the goat! - and then I want one and - I'm the only person in the dog-gone house that's got the slightest bit of consideration for other people and thoughtfulness and consider there may be others that may want to use the doggone bathroom after me and consider -"

He was pitching the chill abominations into the bath-tub, pleased by the vindictiveness of that desolate flapping sound; and in the midst his wife serenely trotted in, observed serenely, "Why Georgie dear, what are you doing? Are you going to wash out the towels? Why, you needn't wash out the towels. Oh, Georgie, you didn't go and use the guest-towel, did you?"

It is not recorded that he was able to answer.

For the first time in weeks he was sufficiently roused by his wife to look at her.

— Sinclair Lewis, *Babbitt*, 1922

Shortly afterwards Bunny came in and hit Meredith quite sharply on the shoulder with his umbrella. He woke stupefied, flicking his tongue over his parched lips like a reptile.

"Go to the kitchens," Bunny ordered Stella. "Ask the waiter with the dent in his forehead to give you a bucketful of ice cubes and three or four napkins. Tell him to send up black coffee and aspirins. And when you've done that go home and stay there until it's time for the evening performance."

— Beryl Bainbridge, *An Awfully Big Adventure*, 1989

"No matter what, you always feel bad in the morning, anyway. To drink or not to drink, I say what's the difference? Go to bed at eight o'clock or stay up all night, the next day you'll still feel the way the billy goat smells."

— Jesse Hill Ford, *The Liberation of Lord Byron Jones*, 1964/1965

M. Laruelle poured himself another *anis*. He was drinking *anis* because it reminded him of absinthe. A deep flush had suffused his face, and his hands trembled slightly over the bottle, from whose label a florid demon brandished a pitchfork at him.

"— I meant to persuade him to go away and get *déalcoholisé*," Dr. Virgil was saying. He stumbled over the word in French and continued in English. "But I was so sick myself that day after the ball that I suffer, physical, really. That is very bad, for we doctors must comport ourselves like apostles. You remember we played tennis that day too. Well, after I lookèd the Consul in his garden I sended a boy down to see if he would come for a few minutes and knock my door, I would appreciate it to him, if not, please write me a note, if drinking have not killed him already."

M. Laruelle smiled.

"But they have gone," the other went on, "and yes, I think to ask you too that day if you had lookèd him at his house."

"He was at my house when you telephoned, Arturo."

"Oh, I know, but we got so horrible drunkness that night before, so *perfectamente borracho*, that it seems to me, the Consul is as sick as I am." Dr. Virgil shook his head. "Sickness is not only in body, but in that part used to be call: soul. Poor your friend he spend his money on earth in such continuous tragedies."

— Malcolm Lowry, *Under the Volcano*, 1947

"Philip Banter," he said to himself, "you are in a bad way."

He stood on the corner of Madison Avenue and Fiftieth Street blinking his aching eyes against the mild winter sunshine. He was trying to decide whether to cross the street or not. If he crossed the street, he would be confronted by the entrance to his office building and he would have to go through the revolving door and into the elevator and up to his office. But if he did not cross the street...if he turned right instead...and walked down the side street a few doors...he would find a bar and have himself a drink. Just one little drink, no more. That was what he needed. Just one little drink.

He did not cross the street. He turned right and walked to the bar and went inside and sat in the rear booth and ordered a double shot of rye whisky when the waiter came. That was what he needed. That would get it over quickly. That would clear his head.

In a few minutes the ache that had gripped his eyeballs had relaxed until it was only an occasional flickering, the slightest hint of pressure. He found he could think again — he could look straight at things — the bar mirror was what he was looking at right then — without flinching. Now everything would be fine if he could just remember what had happened last night.

— John Franklin Bardin, *The Last of Philip Banter*, 1947

Hungover in Philadelphia

※

In Act III of Philip Barry's droll and witty comedy *The Philadelphia Story*, the characters gather in the sitting room of the Lord mansion on the day of Tracy Lord's wedding to George Kittredge. The night before saw excess drinking and personal revelations as well as a drunken dip in the pool. The result is that most of the characters in the following scene, save Tracy's younger sister Dinah, are at least mildly hungover. And forthcoming revelations will make Tracy feel even worse.

Note that, in George Cukor's famous 1940 film, Tracy was played by Katherine Hepburn, Cary Grant played C. K. Dexter Haven, Tracy's first husband with whom she is still in love, James Stewart was tabloid writer Macauley "Mike" Connor and Ruth Hussey appeared as tabloid photographer Liz Imbrie.

When the play premiered at New York's Shubert Theatre the year before, those four characters were played by another impressive cast, respectively, Hepburn, Joseph Cotton, Van Heflin and Shirley Booth.

From Act III, Scene III:

(TRACY comes in from the hall, Right 2, in the dress in which she is to be married. She has a leather-strapped wrist-watch in her hand. DEXTER rises and goes up above sofa. DINAH to back of WILLIE'S chair, Left.)

TRACY. *(Crossing down Right end of sofa)* Hello! Isn't it a fine day, though! Is everyone fine? That's fine! *(Crossing uncertainly Center of sofa. Sits.)* My, I'm hearty.

DEXTER. How are you otherwise? *(Down to upper corner of sofa.)*

TRACY. I don't know what's the matter with me. I must have had too much sun yesterday.

DEXTER. It's awfully easy to get too much.

TRACY. My eyes don't open properly. *(Picks up silver cigarette box from coffee table; looks at eyes)* Please go home, Dext.

DEXTER. Not till we get those eyes open. *(Sits on sofa beside her)*

TRACY. Uncle Willie, good morning.

UNCLE WILLIE. *(Leaning forward)* That remains to be seen.

TRACY. Aren't you here early?

UNCLE WILLIE. Weddings get me out like nothing else.

DINAH. It's nearly half-past twelve. *(Goes Right; sits armchair Right Center)*

TRACY. It can't be.

DINAH. Maybe it can't, but it is.

TRACY. Where - where's Mother?

DINAH. *(Rises)* Do you want her?

TRACY. No, I just wondered.

DINAH. *(Reseats herself)* She's talking with the orchestra, and Father with the minister, and —

TRACY. Doctor Parsons - already?

DINAH. — And Miss Imbrie's gone with her camera to shoot the horses, and Sandy's in his room and — and Mr. Connor, he hasn't come down yet.

DEXTER. And it's Saturday.

TRACY. Thanks loads. It's nice to have things accounted for. *(Passes the hand with the wrist-watch over her eyes, then looks at the watch)* — Only I wonder what this might be?

DEXTER. It looks terribly like a wristwatch.

TRACY. But whose? I found it in my room. I nearly stepped on it.

DINAH. Getting out of bed?

TRACY. Yes. Why?

DINAH. *(Knowingly)* I just wondered. *(Rises and crosses behind* WILLIE'S *chair, Left center)*

TRACY. *(Puts the watch on the table before her)* There's another mystery, Uncle Willie.

UNCLE WILLIE. Mysteries irritate me.

TRACY. I was robbed at your house last night.

UNCLE WILLIE. You don't say.

TRACY. Yes — my bracelet and my engagement ring are missing everywhere.

UNCLE WILLIE. Probably someone's house guest from New York.

(TRACY *nods agreement)*

DEXTER. *(Brings them from his pocket)* Here you are.

TRACY. *(Stares at them, then at him)* - But you weren't at the party!

DEXTER. Wasn't I?

TRACY. Were you?

DEXTER. Don't tell me you don't remember!

TRACY. I — I do now, sort of — but there were such a lot of people.

(DEXTER *gives jewels to her.* TRACY *puts them on table.*)

DEXTER. *(Rises, crossing up behind Right armchair)* You should have taken a quick swim to shake them off. There's nothing like a swim after a late night.

TRACY. — A swim. *(And her eyes grow rounder)*

DEXTER. *(Laughs)* There! Now they're open!

DINAH. *(Crossing a bit to Center)* That was just the beginning — and it was no dream.

DEXTER. *(Glances at her, crossing to WILLIE)* Don't you think, sir, that if you and I went to the pantry at this point — you know: speaking of eye-openers?

UNCE WILLIE. *(Rises and precedes him toward the porch L1)* The only sane remark I've heard this morning. I know a formula that is said to pop the pennies off the eyelids of dead Irishmen. *(Exits Left 1)*

DEXTER. *(Over Left; stops at table)* Oh, Dinah — if conversation drags, you might tell Tracy your dream. *(Exits Left 1)*

TRACY. What did he say?

DINAH. (*Center*) Oh, nothing. (*Crossing in front of sofa. Puts arm on TRACY'S shoulder*) Tray - I hate you to get married and go away.

TRACY. I'll miss you, darling. I'll miss all of you.

DINAH. We'll miss you, too. – It—it isn't like when you married Dexter, and just moved down the road a ways.

TRACY. I'll come back often. It's only Wilkes-Barre.

DINAH. It gripes me.

TRACY. Baby.

(*There is another silence. Finally DINAH speaks:*)

DINAH. (*Sits on upper arm of sofa*) You know I did have the funniest dream about you last night.

TRACY. Did you? What was it?

DINAH. It was terribly interesting, and – and awfully scary, sort of –

TRACY. (*Rises; a step forward*) Do you like my dress, Dinah?

DINAH. Yes, ever so much.

TRACY. (*Rises too quickly, wavers a moment, steadies herself, then moves to the Left 1 door*) It feels awfully heavy. — You'd better rush and get ready yourself. (*Goes Center to Left*)

(MARGARET *enters Right 1.*)

DINAH. You know me. I don't take a minute.

(*VIOLINS off Right tune up.*)

MARGARET. Turn around, Tracy. (TRACY *turns*) Yes, it looks lovely. (*Goes to Center*)

TRACY. (*Left*) What's that — that scratching sound I hear?

MARGARET. (*Center*) The orchestra tuning. Yes — (*Crossing up Right*) I'm glad we decided against the blue one. Where's your father? You know, I feel completely impersonal about all this. I can't quite grasp it. Get dressed, Dinah. (*Goes into the hall, Right 2*)

TRACY. (*Over Left blinks into the sunlight from Left 1*) That sun is certainly bright all right, isn't it?

DINAH. It was up awfully early.

TRACY. Was it?

DINAH. (*Crossing Left center*) Unless I dreamed that, too. — It's supposed to be the longest day of the year or something, isn't it?

TRACY. I wouldn't doubt it for a minute,

DINAH. It was all certainly pretty rooty-tooty. (*Sits Right of table Left*)

TRACY. What was?

DINAH. My dream.

TRACY. (*Crossing below table to Center*) Dinah, you'll have to learn sooner or later that no one is interested in anyone else's dreams. (*Goes to above armchair Right and back of sofa*)

DINAH. — I thought I got up and went over to the window and looked out across the lawn. And guess what I thought I saw coming over out of the woods?

TRACY. (*Back of sofa, then crossing down Right*) I haven't the faintest idea. A skunk?

DINAH. Well, sort of. — It was Mr. Connor.

TRACY. Mr. Connor? (*At lower end of sofa*)

DINAH. Yes — with both arms full of something. And guess what it turned out to be?

TRACY. What?

DINAH. You — and some clothes. (*TRACY turns slowly and looks at her*) Wasn't it funny? It was sort of like as if you were coming from the pool —

TRACY. (*Closes her eyes*) The pool. — I'm going crazy. I'm standing here solidly on my own two hands going crazy — And then what? (*Goes below sofa to Right Center*)

DINAH. Then I thought I heard something outside in the hall, and I went and opened the door a crack and there he was, still coming along with you, puffing like a steam engine. His wind can't be very good.

TRACY. And then what? — (*Goes in Center*)

DINAH. And you were sort of crooning —

TRACY. I never crooned in my life!

DINAH. I guess it just sort of sounded like you were. Then he — guess what?

TRACY. I — couldn't possibly.

DINAH. Then he just sailed into your room with you and — and that scared me so, that I just flew back to bed — or thought I did — and pulled the covers up over my head and layed there shaking and thinking; if *that's* the way it is, why doesn't she marry him instead of old George? And then I must have fallen even faster asleep, because the next thing I knew it was eight o'clock and the typewriter still going.

TRACY. Sandy — typewriter —

DINAH. (*Rises; kneels in chair*) So in a minute I got up and went to your door and peeked in, to make sure you were all right — and guess what?

TRACY. *(Agonized)* What?

DINAH. You were. He was gone by then.

TRACY. Gone? Of course he was gone — he was never there!

DINAH. I know, Tracy.

TRACY. Well! I should certainly hope you did! *(Goes over Right to armchair; sits)*

DINAH. *(Rises, following* TRACY*)* I'm certainly glad I do, because if I didn't and if in a little while I heard Doctor Parsons saying, "If anyone knows any just cause or reason why these two should not be united in holy matrimony" — *I* just wouldn't know what to do. — And it was all only a dream. (Goes up center slowly to stool)

TRACY. Naturally!

DINAH. I know. Dexter said so straight off. — But isn't it funny, though —

TRACY. (Half turning) Dexter!

DINAH. *(Crossing down Center to Left of TRACY)* Yes. — He said —

TRACY. *(Grabbing DINAH'S arm)* You told Dexter all that?

DINAH. Not a word. Not one single word. — But you know how quick he is.

TRACY. Dinah Lord — you little fiend; how can you —?

SETH. (*Enters from the hall Right 2. Back of sofa*) Tracy, the next time you marry, choose a different Man of God, will you? This one wears me out. (*Goes to the Right 1 door; looks in*) Good heavens! — Dinah! Get into your clothes! You look like a tramp, (*Is about to go out again Right 2. Tracy's voice stops him*)

DINAH. I'm going. (*Goes up to corner Right*)

TRACY. Father!

SETH. (*Turns to her. Crossing down Center*) Yes, Tracy?

TRACY. I'm glad you came back. I'm glad you're here.

SETH. Thank you, child.

TRACY. I'm sorry — I'm truly sorry I'm a disappointment to you.

SETH. I never said that, daughter — and I never will. (*Looks at her for a moment, touches her arm, then turns abruptly and goes out Right 2*) Where's your mother? Where's George?

MIKE. (*Comes in from the porch Left 1. Crossing in front of table Left, puts out cigarette*) Good morning.

TRACY. Oh, hello!

MIKE. I was taking the air. I like it, but it doesn't like me. — Hello, Dinah.

DINAH. *(Step toward him to armchair Left Center)* How do you do?

TRACY. *(Right Center)* Did — did you have a good sleep?

MIKE. *(Crossing in Center to Tracy)* Wonderful. How about you?

TRACY. Marvelous. Have you ever seen a handsomer day?

MIKE. Never. What did it set you back?

(DINAH moves down Center.)

TRACY. I got it for nothing, for being a good girl.

MIKE. Good.

(There is a brief silence. They look at DINAH. Finally:)

DINAH. *(Crossing sofa to door Right 1)* I'm going, don't worry.

TRACY. Why should you?

DINAH. *(Over Right at lower end of sofa; turns to them)* I guess you must have things you wish to discuss.

TRACY. "Things to —"? What are you talking about?

DINAH. Only remember it's getting late. *(Gingerly she opens the Right 1 door a crack, and peers in)* Some of them are in already. My, they look solemn. *(Closes door, and moves toward the hall up Right 2)* I'll be ready when you are. *(Exits Right 2)*

TRACY. *(Crossing Left)* She's always trying to make situations. *(Front of table. MIKE arm of Right Center chair; laughs)* — How's your work coming — are you doing us up brown?

MIKE. I've — somehow I've lost my angle.

TRACY. How do you mean, Mike?

MIKE. I've just got so damn tolerant all at once, I doubt if I'll ever be able to write another line.

TRACY. *(Laughs)* You are a fellah, Mike.

MIKE. Or the mug of the world: I don't know.

TRACY. When you're at work you ought to be doing, you'll see that tolerance — What's the matter with your chin?

MIKE. Does it show?

TRACY. A little. What happened?

MIKE. I guess I just stuck it out too far.

TRACY. — Into a door, in the dark?

MIKE. That's it. *(Rises, crossing in Left)* Are *you* — are you all right, Tracy?

TRACY. Me? Of course. Why shouldn't I be?

MIKE. That was a flock of wine we put away.

TRACY. (Crossing below him to armchair Right Center) I never felt better in my life.

MIKE. That's fine. That's just daisy.

TRACY. (Sits in armchair Right Center) I — I guess we're lucky both of us have such good heads.

MIKE. Yes, I guess. (Goes to near her)

TRACY. It must be awful for people who — you know — get up and make speeches or — or try to start a fight — or, you know — misbehave in general.

MIKE. It certainly must.

TRACY. It must be — some sort of hidden weakness coming out.

MIKE. Weakness? I'm not so sure of that. (Chuckles)

TRACY. (She imitates him. Rises, crossing Center to Left) Anyhow, I had a simply wonderful evening. I hope you enjoyed it too.

MIKE. (Right Center) I enjoyed the last part of it.

TRACY. Really? Why? — why especially the last?

MIKE. Are you asking me, Tracy?

TRACY. *(Front of armchair Left Center)* Oh, you mean the swim! — We did swim, and so forth, didn't we?

MIKE. We swam, and so forth.

TRACY. *(Turns to him suddenly. At table Left Center)* Mike —

MIKE. *(Beside her)* You darling, darling girl —

TRACY. Mike!

MIKE. What can I say to you? Tell em, darling —

TRACY. *(Crossing below him to upper corner of sofa)* Not anything — don't say anything. And especially not "Darling."

MIKE. Never in this world will I ever forget you.

TRACY. — Not anything, I said.

MIKE. *(Crossing in back of armchair Right center to her)* You're going to go through with it, then —

TRACY. Through with what?

MIKE. The wedding.

TRACY. Why — why shouldn't I?

MIKE. Well, you see, I've made funny discovery: that in spite of the fact that someone's up from the bottom, he may be quite a heel. And that even though someone else's born to the purple, he still may be quite a guy. — Hell, I'm only saying what you said last night!

TRACY. I said a lot of things last night, it seems. (*Goes down*)

MIKE. (*After a moment*) All right, no dice. But understand: also no regrets about last night.

TRACY. (*Backs away to Right*) Why should I have?

MIKE. (*Crossing below sofa to her*) That's it! That's the stuff; you're wonderful. You're aces, Tracy.

TRACY. (*Backing away from him to lower corner sofa*) You don't know what I mean! I'm asking you — tell me straight out — tell me the reason why I should have any — (*But she cannot finish. Her head drops*) No — don't. — (*Goes Center*) Just tell me — what time is it?

MIKE. (*Glancing at his wrist*) What's happened to my wrist watch?

TRACY. (*Stops, frozen; speaks without turning*) Why? Is it broken?

MIKE. (*Front of sofa*) It's gone. I've lost it somewhere.

TRACY. (*Left Center. After a moment*) I can't tell you how extremely sorry I am to hear that. (*Goes to table*)

MIKE. Oh, well — I'd always just as soon not know the time.

TRACY. *(Her back to him)* There on the table —

MIKE. — What is? *(Goes to the coffee table; finds the watch)* Well, for the love of — ! Who found it? I'll give a reward, or something. *(Straps the watch on his wrist)*

TRACY. I don't think any reward will be expected.

DEXTER. *(Comes in Left 1, cocktail glass in hand)* Now, then! This medicine indicated in cases of — *(Stops at the sight of MIKE)* Hello, Connor. How are you?

MIKE. *(At sofa, crossing Left Center)* About as you'd think. — Is that for me?

DEXTER. *(Over Left)* For Tracy. — Why? Would you like one?

MIKE. *(Crossing to Left)* I would sell my grandmother for a drink — and you know how I love my grandmother.

(TRACY goes up front of sofa)

DEXTER. Uncle Willie's around in the pantry, doing weird and wonderful things. Just say I said, One of the same.

MIKE. *(Moves toward the porch and below table to Left)* Is it all right if I say Two?

DEXTER. That's between you and your grandmother. *(MIKE exits Left 1)* — And find Liz! *(TRACY sits armchair Right Center. DEXTER goes to TRACY with the drink*) Doctor's orders, Tray.

TRACY. What is it?

DEXTER. Just the juice of a few flowers.

TRACY. (*Takes the glass and looks at it. Drinks*) Peppermint —

DEXTER. — White. — And one other simple ingredient. It's called a stinger. It removes the sting.

Watch Other People Suffer

In January 2002, the Internet Movie Database conducted a poll asking site users, "Which movie contains the best hangover scene?" The responses indicate a not-too-surprising shortness of memory at best and a rather disappointing ignorance of cinema history at worst since, with one laudable exception, all the films were made after 1965. In descending order, the top online vote-getters were:

A League of Their Own
Leaving Las Vegas
Die Hard: With a Vengeance
Kingpin
The Philadelphia Story (see previous chapter)
True Grit
The Morning After
The Goodbye Girl
Harper
The Cowboys

For those who wish to take a more in-depth look at the self-inflicted suffering of others, here are a few other films to look for. With the exception of two or three, these movies are all from a period that was less puritanical when it came to drinking to excess. Somehow hangovers are more charming in black and white.

Breakfast of Champions
Cabaret
The Hangover (1931)
The Hangover (1956 - renamed Female Jungle)
Hangover Square (1945)
The Thin Man
The Tender Trap
Teacher's Pet
The African Queen (1951)
The Big Hangover (1950)
Nothing Sacred
Night After Night
The Nutty Professor (Jerry Lewis version)
Remember Last Night (1935)
Suspcion. Based on Francis Iles' famous crime novel *Before the Fact*, this 1940 Alfred Hitchcock thriller opens with a painfully hungover Johnny Aysgarth (Cary Grant) meeting his future wife (Joan Fontaine) in a railway carriage.

Writers and Hangovers

"I have the villain of a headache, my eyes are
two piss holes in the sand, my tongue is
fish-and-chip paper."

— Dylan Thomas, *The Collected Letters*

Neko What's your favourite way to get a hangover?

Richard There are so many wonderful ways to
O'Brien achieve the perfect hangover. Mixing your
drinks is a fairly safe bet. I suggest you start
with a couple of beers, then hit the red
wine, then you swap to something with a
couple of shots in it — Vodka's cool — and
then onto the brandy, with a dash of port
in it. Enjoy.

— Interview with Richard O'Brien, Actor and
author of *The Rocky Horror Picture Show*, Virgin.
net chat

The tempo of the city had changed sharply. The uncertainties of 1920 were drowned in a steady golden roar and many of our friends had grown wealthy. But the restlessness of New York in 1927 approached hysteria. The parties were bigger - those of Condé Nast, for example, rivaled in their way the fabled balls of the nineties; the pace was faster - the catering to dissipation set an example to Paris; the shows were broader, the buildings were higher, the morals were looser and the liquor was cheaper; but all these benefits did not really minister to much delight. Young people wore out early - they were hard and languid at twenty-one and save for Peter Arno none of them contributed anything new; perhaps Peter Arno and his collaborators said everything there was to say about the boom days in New York that couldn't be said by a jazz band. Many people who were not alcoholics were lit up four days out of seven, and frayed nerves were strewn everywhere; groups were held together by a generic nervousness and the hangover became a part of the day as well allowed-for as the Spanish siesta. Most of my friends drank too much - the more they were in tune to the times the more they drank. And as effort *per se* had no dignity against the mere bounty of those days in New York, a depreciatory word was found for it: a successful programme became a racket - I was in the literary racket.

> — F. Scott Fitzgerald, "My Lost City," first published in *The Crack-Up*, edited by Edmund Wilson, 1945

| Interviewers: | And what time of the day do you find best for working? |
| Styron: | The afternoon. I like to stay up late at night and get drunk and sleep late. I wish I could break the habit but I can't. The afternoon is the only time I have left and I try to use it to the best advantage, with a hangover. |

— From *The Paris Review* interview of William Styron, 1956, interview conducted by Peter Matthiessen and George Plimpton

I had one of those heartbeat hangovers where every pump of blood sent a hammer of pain to my head.

Mae was being very good and gave me coffee and eggs and tomato juice and aspirin, and I managed to shower and shave under my own power.

An expense-account taxi took me downtown to the White House. The guards at the gate glanced at my identification and waved me on. It should have been a proud moment—my first day on the job in the Executive Mansion—but I felt like hell. It wasn't only the hangover, which had begun to recede to a dull throb. It was the disenchantment with the whole picture. Instead of walking in with head high I sort of shuffled in, looking at my feet, and almost bumped into a man in the lobby.

— Richard Wilson, *30-Day Wonder*

He awoke to the tune of a beautiful hangover. He gulped seven glasses of water and staggered to the shower. Fifteen minutes of iced needles and some coffee brought him part way back to his own, cheerful self. He headed down the hall toward the elevator.

— George O. Smith, *Venus Equilateral*

I have always lived violently, drunk hugely, eaten too much or not at all, slept around the clock or missed two nights of sleeping, worked too hard and too long in glory, or slobbed for a time in utter laziness. I've lifted, pulled, chopped, climbed, made love with joy and taken my hangovers as a consequence, not as a punishment.

— John Steinbeck, *Travels with Charley*

There is no night life in Spain. They stay up late but they get up late. That is not night life. That is delaying the day. Night life is when you get up with a hangover in the morning. Night life is when everybody says what the hell and you do not remember who paid the bill. Night life goes round and round and you look at the wall to make it stop. Night life comes out of a bottle and goes into a jar. If you think how much are the drinks it is not night life.

— Ernest Hemingway, *88 Poems*

You can have a hangover from other things than alcohol. I had one from women. Women made me sick.

— Raymond Chandler, *The Big Sleep*

I like to change liquor stores frequently because the clerks got to know your habits if you went in night and day and bought huge quantities. I could feel them wondering why I wasn't dead yet and it made me uncomfortable. They probably weren't thinking any such thing, but then a man gets paranoid when he has 300 hangovers a year.

— Charles Bukowski, *Women*

P.S. ~ in re: *Oui*'s request for "my hangover cure" — it's 12 amyl nitrites (one box), in conjunction with as many beers as necessary.

— Hunter S. Thompson

Deadly Hangovers

When I opened my eyes I was sure they were going to fall out of my head and start rolling across the floor like a couple of marbles. The pillow felt as if it had been cooked in butter. I looked at the time. It was only eight o'clock, and I knew that if I could sleep four or five hours more I might get over the notion I was going to die. But my head was full of worms, those mean little gnawing worms that you can hear gnawing their way through a tree-trunk or through your head when you've been drinking as much as we had drunk the night before. We had had everything, all the way from Scotch to Pernod and back with way stations of Amer Picon and, for no valid reason, some Danziger Goldwasser. I also remembered some brandy out of a bottle shaped like a crown and marked "Très Vielle, Âge Inconnu." I nudged Carlotta.

"How do you feel?" I asked.

"The kerchief didn't match the bottom," she said. "That was the top."

I nudged her again. This time she awoke.

"How do you feel?" I asked once more.

"Oh my God, it's you," she said. "And if all you wanted to know is how do I feel, you could have left me a note which I could read when I woke up."

"You're talking too much," I said.

Carlotta stretched and tried to sit up in bed. Then a look came over her face that must be like the look that comes over a man's face just when the executioner springs the trap. I couldn't help laughing.

"I had a funny dream last night," I said. "Oh, it was a horrible dream!"

Carlotta sat straight up in bed and this time she stayed sitting up. I expected to see her head fly off her neck and go floating around the room; and I wondered whether I should be able to poke it and it would fizzle like a balloon and come down, and I would be able to catch it and fasten it back. But her head stayed on and she sat with a glassy look in her eyes.

"I had a funny dream too," she said. "Something very screwy."

"It was screwy all right," I said. "It scared the hell out of me."

"It was horrible," Carlotta said. "Simply horrible."

I took a drink of water and then I wished I hadn't.

"Say, I just thought of something," I said. Carlotta was still sitting up in bed looking baffled. "It's a funny thing we both had the same dream."

"I was just thinking of that, too. But I suppose anything can happen when you're drunk."

"Sure, but I never had the same dream as anyone else before."

"Neither did I," Carlotta said. "But I don't even remember what the dream was except that it was screwy."

"That's another funny thing," I said. "I don't remember it either. It was screwy and horrible."

We both lay back in bed, very carefully. The walls kept looking as if they were going to bulge and then buckle and let the ceiling fall down on our heads.

"I've got that milk-bottle feeling," Carlotta said. "I feel like a fly flying around in a milk-bottle. The world I live in is a milk-bottle and I'm a fly flying around in it."

"I feel like a green bubble," I said. "Once I saw a dead dog at the bottom of a well. I was walking along and I came to this deserted well, be and there was a dog who had drowned in it. He was floating on the water with his paws stuck up stiff. His belly was all swollen up. I threw a stone down at him and broke his belly and he sank. Well, just as he sank, a bubble came up and burst in the green scum on the water. My head feels like that bubble just at the moment it burst."

Carlotta groaned.

"You told me that once before," she said. "It's good, but it's too complicated."

"So I've heard," I said. "I dare you to get up."

"Oh, go to hell," Carlotta said. "It's too early. There won't be anybody in this house up before noon. I don't see why you don't go to sleep."

"I'm not sleepy," I said. "I can't sleep."

"Neither am I." She yawned and stretched under the covers and stuck one foot out. "It must belong to me," she said, "because it wiggles when I want it to." She groaned some more. "God, I smell like a bar-rag. I feel like something you find under a rock. I feel - "

I didn't listen any more. I knew it was an epic simile she was going to compound, which all comes from reading Homer. Carlotta is sometimes a very dumb girl, but she can still read Homer. I swung my feet out over the floor and waited for it to come up and meet them. It did, like a deck of a ship in heavy weather. Then I walked across the floor, which was leaping nimbly under me, to a little bar in the corner of the room. We were staying at Jack Huling's and Jack was thoughtful about such things. He killed you and cured you and then he killed you again. Carlotta got up and went to the bathroom. She hadn't put her slippers on. I was always giving her hell for running around in her bare feet. She would catch some kind of disease some time.

"Want a drink?" I asked.

"It might make my ears feel funny," Carlotta said. "They feel pretty funny now."

She got back into bed.

"I know how they feel," I said. "They feel as if they were full of mud."

"No, they feel as if they were full of mud that was full of little clams all opening and closing their shells."

I made a highball and carried it over to her. She held it up to the light to see how strong I had made it. Then she looked at my drink.

"You made yours stronger than mine," she said.

"I put exactly the same in both."

"Well, they're not strong enough."

I sweetened both drinks and we drank them. They didn't make us feel any better. I made us another drink.

"I want some temporary death," Carlotta said. "Dear God, please send me a small order of temporary death, just a side dish of temporary death, please, God."

We drank our second drinks.

— Adam Hobhouse, *The Hangover Murders*, 1935

I opened my eyes and they immediately cringed shut again under the impact of bright merciless sunlight streaming in through the bedroom window. The chunk of lead sitting precariously on top of my shoulders protested violently when I lifted it a couple of inches, then fought back with a succession of sharp stabbing pains. Somehow I managed to get up into a sitting position and hold my head in my hands, while somebody tried real hard to knock it down flush with my shoulders, using an outsize sledgehammer. It had been one hell of a party, I dimly remembered.

By the time I had taken a long shower, a careful, careful shave, and had brushed my teeth five times, I didn't feel any better. Worse, if anything, because those dim memories of the night before were coming back in sharp focus. They didn't return in any kind of sequence, just in isolated pictures like stills from some horror movie. I suddenly remembered the little fat guy who said he was going out onto the terrace for a little fresh air, and it wasn't until he had one leg over the windowsill that I remembered my apartment doesn't have a terrace - just a sheer drop of thirteen floors down onto Central Park West.

There was the real wild redhead with a kind of Grand Canyon cleavage - I winced at the memory! - the one who had climbed all over me in the kitchen and said not to worry just because her husband was a professional wrestler, so I didn't - right up until the moment he walked in on us a couple of minutes later. My back gave a painful twinge and I idly wondered just what it was I had slammed against after he threw me across the room. Then there was...but why go on? I figured it would only make me some kind of masochist if I kept trying to remember any more of the party, so I decided to concentrate on getting dressed. It only took around fifteen minutes, after I quit trying to knot a tie with fingers that shook like a bongo player busy limbering up for a jazz session someplace. Then I made the tragic mistake of walking into the living room, hell - it looked more like the city dump two minutes after the hurricane hit.

The merciless sunlight was strong enough to pierce the thick haze of stale tobacco smoke and reveal everything in harsh, terrifying detail. What looked like a thousand dirty glasses were scattered around the room, some still half full of liquor, and a couple had cigarette butts floating in them. All the ashtrays were overflowing, so some of my more thoughtful guests had simply ground their butts straight into the rug. But, still and all, the furniture was intact - even if a three-legged table would be a little tricky to live with - and intuition told me it must have been the professional wrestler who had wrenched both doors clean off the buffet. The armchairs looked as good as new, except for the one with the big cigarette burn right through the upholstery, and I figured the couch would be okay when it had been yanked back onto its feet again. I walked unsteadily across to it, bent down to get a good grip on one end, then froze.

Oh no! my mind whimpered. You would figure something would have been left behind after a wild party, but this was ridiculous. Somewhere in Manhattan there was a brand-new female dwarf running loose. How in hell anybody could forget their own legs was beyond the scope of my blurred mind right then.

— Carter Brown (aka Alan G. Yates), *The Black Lace Hangover*, 1966

Royce wasn't sure what woke him up so early the next morning, but was surprised that anything short of a rattlesnake with its tongue in his ear could do it. The hangover was bad, but it was a little better than the day's prospects, like most days. This information had long since become subliminal, and usually allowed him to drink long and hard, sleep long and hard, booze and snooze. It wasn't until standing at the kitchen sink and draining his second tall glass of tap water that he realized what must have happened.

He could see the driveway and the front end of his pickup from where he stood, off to the side of the house. Red plastic lay on the cement below the bumper, where he'd crushed her taillight lenses earlier this morning. Her car was gone. But shards of white glass mingled with the red ones on the pavement, and, without leaning over too much, he could see she'd done a little work on the truck on the way out. It would be just like her to notice the broken taillights right off, the paranoid bitch. Tit for tat, a headlight for a taillight lens...

An eye for an eye. Punitive reciprocity.

He had a very bad headache. Sound and light fired through his brain the way deep, mile-long cracks shoot through pack ice.

She had destroyed the kitchen, or rather, most of the stuff in it. Pieces of glass and crockery were everywhere; he had to put his shoes on to get safely to the sink. She'd even torn an upper cabinet door half off its hinges, and one piece of Formica showed the traces of being clawed by desperate fingernails, or a fork. Looking at the room, he could practically hear the Wagner in her mind. If the cops had walked in at that moment, they'd have had him under a hot light in no time, trying to sweat out the location of Pamela's body.

Indeed, he wished he did know where she was buried.

But that kind of thinking had never gotten him anywhere and never would. Or, more precisely, he'd never followed up on it. And never would.

Right?

He drew a third glass of water and took it with him to his desk in the library. There he chased down some aspirin. The answering machine tape was blank, as it almost always was. Business was bad; social contacts were nonexistent. The conversation he'd had in the bar on the way home last night was the longest he'd talked to anyone in a long time without shouting at them. Had that been just last night? This morning?

He looked at the clock. A quarter to twelve. This morning, just barely. It had been a very long one.

— Jim Nisbet, *Lethal Injection*, 1987

Nor did Santiago Nasar recognize the omen. He had slept little and poorly, without getting undressed, and he woke up with a headache and a sediment of copper stirrup on his palate, and he interpreted them as the natural havoc of the wedding revels that had gone on until after midnight. Furthermore: all the many people he ran into after leaving his house at five minutes past six and until he was carved up like a pig an hour later remembered him as being a little sleepy but in a good mood, and he remarked to all of them in a casual way that it was a very beautiful day. No one was certain if he was referring to the state of the weather. Many people coincided in recalling that it was a radiant morning with a sea breeze coming in through the banana groves, as was to be expected in a fine February of that period. But most agreed that the weather was funereal, with a cloudy, low sky and the thick smell of still waters, and that at the moment of the misfortune a thin drizzle was falling like the one Santiago Nasar had seen in his dream grove. I was recovering from the wedding revels in the apostolic lap of María Alejandrina Cervantes, and I only awakened with the clamour of the alarm bells, thinking they had turned them loose in honour of the bishop.

— Gabriel García Marquez, *Chronicle of a Death Foretold*, Translated by Gregory Rabassa, 1983

My eyes were still wooly from the night before and I didn't want to move my head too quickly for fear my brains would spring out like watchworks.

— Loren D. Estleman, *Whisky River*, 1990

A Selected Bibliography

Non-Fiction (more or less)

Adams, John F.   *An Essay on Brewing, Vintage and Distillation Together with Selected Remedies for Hangover Melancholia or How to Make Booze.* Garden City: Doubleday, 1970.

Benady, Alex   *Little Book of Hangover Cures.* Appletree Press, 1997.

Clayton, David and

David Langdon   *Wake up and Die.* London: Allan Wingate, 1952.

Coppolino, Carl & *Billion Dollar Hangover.* New
Carmela   York; AS Barnes, 1965.

Davis, Hassoldt.   *Bonjour, Hangover!* New York: Duell, Sloan and Pearce, 1958.

Freud, Clement   *Hangovers.* London: Sheldon Press, 1981.

Gillespie Jr., James   *Hangover 1936.* New York: Gal-
Stuart.   leon Press, 1937.

Karpman, Benjamin. *Hangover: A Critical Study in the Psychodynamics of Alcoholism.* Springfield, Illinois: Charles C. Thomas, 1957.

Lennane, Jean. *Alcohol the National Hangover.* North Sydney, Australia: Thomas and Unwin, 1992.

Maultsby Jr. MD, Maxie C. *A Million Dollars for Your Hangover: the Illustrated Guide for the New Self-Help Alcoholic Treatment Method.* Lexington, Kentucky: Rational Self-Help Books, 1978.

Meaker, M.J. (Marijane) *A Guide to the Hangover.* New York: Dell Publishing Co., 1962.

Outerbridge, David *The Hangover Handbook: The Definitive Guide to the Causes and Cures of Mankind's Oldest Affliction.* New York: Harmony Books, 1981.

Ogilvy, Ian. *A Slight Hangover.*

Raouth, Jonathan *The Hangover Book: Prevention, Preparation, Treatment and Cure.* Wolfe Publishing, 1967.

Scrivener, Jane *The Quick-Fix Hangover Detox: 99 Ways to Feel 100 Times Better.* Judy Piatkus Publishers, 2001.

Smedley, Jack and Jill. *The Hangover Cookbook.* New English Library, 1970.

Taylor, Richard *By the Dawn's Ugly Light - A Pictorial Study of the Hangover.* New York: Henry Holt, 1953.

Toper, Andy	*The Wrath of Grapes or The Hangover Companion*. London: Souvenir Press, 1966.
Van Oudtshoorn, Nic	*Hangover Handbook: 101 Cures for Humanity's Oldest Malady*. Memphis, Tennessee: Mustang Publishing, 1993.
Walther, Anne N., MS	*Divorce Hangover: A Step-by-Step Prescription for Creating a Bright Future after Your Marriage Ends*. New York: Pocket Books, 1991.

Fiction (in some cases, despite the titles, having nothing whatsoever to do with that morning-after crapulous feeling)

Bitz, Gregory	*War Hangover*. Angel Wing Press, 1987.
Brown, Carter.	*The Black Lace Hangover*. Sydney: Horwitz, 1966.
Goonewardene, James.	*Tribal Hangover*. New Delhi: Penguin India, 1995.
Hamilton, Patrick.	*Hangover Square or The Man with Two Minds*. London: Constable, 1941.
Hobhouse, Alan.	*The Hangover Murders*. New York: Alfred A. Knopf, 1935.
Kenne, Alex	*Hangover*. New York: Farrar, Straus and Co., 1948.

Kennedy, X.J.	*Hangover Mass (and other poems)*. Cleveland: Bits Press, 1984.
Lief, Max.	*Hangover*. New York: Horace Liveright, 1929. (Republished as Wild Parties)
Redd, Louise.	*Hangover Soup*. Boston: Little Brown, 1999.
Rohmer, Sax.	*Hangover House*. New York, Random House, 1949.
Sargeson, Frank.	*The Hangover*. London: MacGibbon & Kee, 1967.
Ward, Tony	*Lust Hangover*. Candlelight, 1964.
Williams, J.X.	*Passion Hangover*. Corinth Publications, 1965.

Credits

Every reasonable effort has been made to determine copyright owners for material contained in this book.

In the case of any errors or omissions, these are wholly unintentional and the Publisher will be pleased to make suitable acknowledgments in future printings.

Bill Pronzini, *Jackpot*

Ronald Harwood, *The Guilt Merchants*

R.F. Delderfield, *The Spring Madness of Mr. Sermon*

Fay and Michael Kanin, *Teacher's Pet*

Alexander Pushkin, *The Captain's Daughter and Other Stories*

C.S. Forester, *The African Queen*

James Agee, *Screenplay for The African Queen* by C.S. Forester

Peter Robinson, *In a Dry Season*

When the Sacred Gin Mill Closes, by Lawrence Block. Used by permission of the author.

Hangover Soup by Louise Redd, copyright © 1999. Reprinted by permission of Little, Brown, an imprint of Hachette Book Group, Inc.

From *Under the Volcano* by Malcolm Lowry. Copyright (c) 1947 by Malcolm Lowry. Copyright renewed 1975 by Margerie Lowry. Introduction copyright (c) 1965 by Harper & Row, Publishers, Inc. Used by permission of HarperCollins Publishers.

Hubert Selby Jr., *Last Exit to Brooklyn*

Robert Penn Warren, *All the King's Men*

Piece of Cake, by Derek Robinson. Used by permission of the author.

Dashiell Hammett, *The Thin Man*

George Orwell, *Down and Out in Paris and London*

Max Webster, "Hangover"

Max Lief, *Hangover* (Republished as *Wild Parties*)

George Orwell, *Animal Farm*